797,885 Books
are available to read at

www.ForgottenBooks.com

Forgotten Books' App
Available for mobile, tablet & eReader

ISBN 978-1-331-59516-8
PIBN 10210499

This book is a reproduction of an important historical work. Forgotten Books uses state-of-the-art technology to digitally reconstruct the work, preserving the original format whilst repairing imperfections present in the aged copy. In rare cases, an imperfection in the original, such as a blemish or missing page, may be replicated in our edition. We do, however, repair the vast majority of imperfections successfully; any imperfections that remain are intentionally left to preserve the state of such historical works.

Forgotten Books is a registered trademark of FB &c Ltd.
Copyright © 2015 FB &c Ltd.
FB &c Ltd, Dalton House, 60 Windsor Avenue, London, SW19 2RR.
Company number 08720141. Registered in England and Wales.

For support please visit www.forgottenbooks.com

1 MONTH OF FREE READING

at

www.ForgottenBooks.com

By purchasing this book you are eligible for one month membership to ForgottenBooks.com, giving you unlimited access to our entire collection of over 700,000 titles via our web site and mobile apps.

To claim your free month visit:

www.forgottenbooks.com/free210499

* Offer is valid for 45 days from date of purchase. Terms and conditions apply.

English
Français
Deutsche
Italiano
Español
Português

www.forgottenbooks.com

Mythology Photography **Fiction** Fishing Christianity **Art** Cooking Essays Buddhism Freemasonry Medicine **Biology** Music **Ancient Egypt** Evolution Carpentry Physics Dance Geology **Mathematics** Fitness Shakespeare **Folklore** Yoga Marketing **Confidence** Immortality Biographies Poetry **Psychology** Witchcraft Electronics Chemistry History **Law** Accounting **Philosophy** Anthropology Alchemy Drama Quantum Mechanics Atheism Sexual Health **Ancient History** **Entrepreneurship** Languages Sport Paleontology Needlework Islam **Metaphysics** Investment Archaeology Parenting Statistics Criminology **Motivational**

MINIATURE IN "BOOK OF HOURS."
Jacqueline kneeling at the right of the Virgin.

A·MEDIAEVAL·PRINCESS
BEING A TRUE RECORD OF THE
CHANGING FORTUNES WHICH
BROUGHT DIVERS TITLES
TO JACQUELINE
COUNTESS OF HOLLAND
TOGETHER WITH AN ACCOUNT
OF HER CONFLICT WITH
PHILIP DUKE OF BURGUNDY
(1401 · 1436)

BY RUTH PUTNAM
HONORARY MEMBER OF THE
'MAATSCHAPPIJ VAN NEDERLANDSCHE
LETTERKUNDE' AT LEYDEN
AUTHOR OF WILLIAM THE SILENT ETC.

G·P PUTNAM'S SONS
NEW YORK
LONDON
1904

A MEDIAEVAL PRINCESS

BEING A TRUE RECORD OF THE CHANGING FORTUNES WHICH BROUGHT DIVERS TITLES TO JACQUELINE COUNTESS OF HOLLAND TOGETHER WITH AN ACCOUNT OF HER CONFLICT WITH PHILIP DUKE OF BURGUNDY (1401 · 1436)

BY RUTH PUTNAM
HONORARY MEMBER OF THE
'MAATSCHAPPIJ VAN NEDERLANDSCHE LETTERKUNDE' AT LEYDEN
AUTHOR OF WILLIAM THE SILENT ETC.

G·P·PUTNAM'S SONS
NEW YORK
LONDON
1904

7555

COPYRIGHT, 1904
BY
RUTH PUTNAM

Published, June, 1904

The Knickerbocker Press, New York

A woman whose gracious personality has influenced many maidens of the nineteenth and a few of the twentieth century, once listened with pleasant interest to this story of a less fortunate damsel of long ago. In memory of the first sketch of the narrative this volume is affectionately inscribed to
S. J. L.

PREFACE

ONLY a very audacious romancer would dare to make his heroine pass through more varied fortunes than those actually experienced by Jacqueline, last independent sovereign in Holland, Zealand, and Hainaut. Orphaned at sixteen, no forethought displayed by her father, no efforts of her successive husbands were able to defend her paternal heritage against the rapacity of her kinsmen. From the moment when she assumed the title in 1417, already forlorn and widowed at the very opening of life, it was a foregone conclusion that at last the strongest man among her cousins and uncles, the Duke of Burgundy, should finally set aside her rights and, severing the tie which attached the otherwise autonomous countships to the Empire, sweep them into an expanding circle of territories, a circle whose periphery at last proved overstretched for its strength.

The methods used by Philip of Spain, which led to the sixteenth century revolt of the Netherlands against his domination have been considered in all phases; but the details of the entry of his Burgundian ancestor, Philip the Good, into Holland a century and a half earlier have received scanty notice in English. Yet the story is full of interest in giving a picture of the meeting between the modern and the mediæval worlds. Moreover, Jacqueline's alliances with the Royal Houses of France and of England, the incidents of Imperial and Papal interference in her fortunes, and the way in which her matrimonial ventures brought about international complications make her a striking figure of her times. Her contemporary, Jeanne d'Arc, fought against and was finally conquered by the same men with whom Jacqueline maintained her futile struggle. The peasant girl has received much attention from posterity; the princess, little; and perhaps this account of her and her lost cause may interest those who like to read the footnotes of history.

The authorities whereon the narrative rests are described elsewhere, but here I would make grateful acknowledgment for the cordial assistance in their use given to me at the libraries of Columbia and Cornell Universities, and at the New York Public Library. With every year our historical material grows richer and becomes more available. Governments and learned societies abroad are exerting themselves to publish records and documents while librarians are co-operating with archivists to the great advantage of students.

My warmest thanks are especially due to Dr. Billings and to the various members of his staff at the Astor for unfailing courtesy. I also desire to express my gratitude to Dr. Bijvanck of the Royal Library at The Hague for his kind suggestions, and to Prof. Blok and Dr. Japikse for their aid at various times from across the sea.

R. P.

NEW YORK, April, 1904.

CONTENTS

	PAGE
PREFACE	v

CHAPTER I
DAUGHTER OF HOLLAND (1401–1417) . . .

CHAPTER II
THE HERITAGE (1417) 18

CHAPTER III
THE SECOND MARRIAGE (1418) . . . . .

CHAPTER IV
THE THREE JOHNS (1418–1419) 52

CHAPTER V
DOMESTIC QUARRELS (1419–1420) . . . 60

CHAPTER VI
REFUGE IN HAINAUT (1420) 70

CHAPTER VII
JACQUELINE IN ENGLAND (1421–1424) . . . 84

CHAPTER VIII
SOVEREIGN IN HAINAUT (1424) 112

Contents

	PAGE
CHAPTER IX	
HOPES AND FEARS (1424–1425)	124
CHAPTER X	
IN PRISON AND OUT (1425)	147
CHAPTER XI	
THE COUNTESS MILITANT (1426–1428)	173
CHAPTER XII	
THE LOST CAUSE (1428)	188
CHAPTER XIII	
THE SILENT PARTNER (1428–1433)	213
CHAPTER XIV	
LADY FORESTER (1433–1436)	247
CHAPTER XV	
HER LAST WILL (1436)	262
CHAPTER XVI	
THE LADY AND THE LAND	282
BIBLIOGRAPHY	315
INDEX	323

ILLUSTRATIONS

Jacqueline Kneeling, in Miniature of the Annunciation . . . . . *Frontispiece*

> One of eleven miniatures in a *Book of Hours,* illuminated for Jacqueline after her marriage to Frank van Borselen. In possession of M. le Comte de Murard, France. Described by Léopold Delisle, *Bibliothèque de l' École du Chartes,* 1903, p. 314. Reproduction loaned by Mr. W. G. C. Bijvanck, the Royal Library, The Hague.

William VI of his Name, 27th Count of Holland, of Zealand, and of Friesland, also Count of Hainaut 6

> Gulielmus Bavariæ. Engraver, K. Sichem. *La Grande Chronique de Hollande,* etc. Jean François Le Petit, i., p. 336. Dordrecht, 1601.

Hôtel-de-Ville, Compiègne 12

> *Voyages dans l' ancienne France.* MM. Taylor, Nodier, et de Cailleux, Paris, 1845. *Picardie,* vol. iii.

Retable in Church of St. Waltrude at Mons, XVth Century 22

> *Monuments classés de l'art dans les Pays-Bas.* Van Ysendyck.

Portal at Zutphen. XVth Century . . 30

> *Monuments classés de l'art dans les Pays-Bas.* Van Ysendyck.

Jacqueline's Seal Appended to Document of August 4, 1415, at The Hague. (After the marriage to John, Duke of Touraine.) *Tailpiece* 43

Illustrations

                                                                                                 PAGE

Photo from original preserved in the archives at Lille. Shield shows lilies of France on one half; the arms or Bavaria and the four lions of Holland-Hainaut in the other quarters. *Legend* + sigillū. Jacobe de Bavarie. ducisse et comitesse. Pontiou.

John of Bavaria 36
Soy disant Tuteur de Hollande (Dñs Johannes Bavarie). *La Grande Chronique*, etc., i., p. 358.

John, Duke of Bedford, Kneeling before St. George. 1430 44
Bedford Missal. Photo from original. MS. Add. 18850.

Flood in South Holland, Owing to a Break in the Dikes. 1421 . . 50
[Drawn originally from a description in Scriverii Batav. Illustr., p. 130.] *Vaderlandsche Historie*. Jan Wagenaar, Amsterdam, 1752.

Jacqueline's Seal Appended to Document, June 22, 1417 . . . . *Tailpiece* 51
Photo from original preserved at Lille. Quarterings show arms of France, Bavaria, Dauphiny, and Holland-Hainaut. *Legend:* S. Jaque ducisse. Bavar. dalphīe. vien cōitesse. hanonie. Z. Hollandie.

Portrait of Jacqueline 62
Jacqueline de Bavière; 29th Sovereign in Holland, Zealand, and Friesland, also Countess and Lady of Hainaut. (*Jacoba Bavariæ*) Le Petit, *La Grande Chronique*, etc., i., p. 358.

                            Inscription.
L'amour par quatre fois me mit en mariage,
Et si n'ay sceu pourtant accroistre mon lignage.
Gorrichem i'ay conquis, contre Guillaume Arcklois
En un jour i'ay perdu presques trois mille Anglois.
Pour avoir mon Mary de sa prison delivre
Au Duc des Bourgoingnons tous mes Pays ie livre.
Dix ans regnay en paine : ore avec mon Ayeul
Contente ie repose en un mesme cerceuil.

Illustrations

                                                                    PAGE

Jacqueline's Seal Appended to Document Granting Estates to the Dowager Countess. October 6, 1417 . . . . *Tailpiece* 69

Photo from original preserved at Lille. Shield is inclosed in a hedge whence issue two branches. Quarterings show lilies of France, and the arms of Bavaria, of Dauphiny, and of Holland-Hainaut. *Legend* (S. Jaque) ducisse. Bavar. dalphīe vien. cōitisse Hanonīe. Hollīe. Z. dn̄e.

Portrait of Henry V, after one at Windsor Castle 78

"Heroes of the Nations." From *Henry V*. Frontispiece.

The Poet Lydgate in his Study . . . 86

Contemp. MS. Harleian 2248, British Museum. Photo from original.

Henry V and Catherine of France. 1420 . 92

From an old print. Lenox Library.

Duke Humphrey's Library. Bodleian Library, Oxford 100

Ackerman's *History of Oxford*. London, 1814. ii., 229.

Anne of Burgundy, Duchess of Bedford, Kneeling before the Virgin and Child . 110

Bedford Missal, MS. Add. 18850, British Museum. Photo from original.

Cardinal Beaufort, Bishop of Winchester 122

From a painting in the collection of Horace Walpole.

Twelve-Branched Candelabra Presented to the Citizens of Bois-le-Duc for their Bravery at Braine-le-Comte. 1425 134

Monuments classés, etc.

The Grafenstein at Ghent 148

From *Gent und Tournai*. Henri Hymans, Leipzig, 1902.

	PAGE

The Flight of the Duchess from Ghent. 1425 . 154

From *Algemeene Geschiedenis des Vaderlands.* J. P. Arend, Amsterdam, 1844.

This representation of Jacqueline with her rescuers and the view of the archery festival are excellent examples of numerous fanciful representations of her adventures. Naturally she has been a favourite subject for later-day painters in Holland.

Jacqueline on the Battle-field . . . 174

From *Het Vereenigd Nederland.* J. P. Martinet, Amsterdam, 1788.

River Fishing . . . . *Tailpiece* 187

From Harleian MS. No. 4374.

Portrait of Henry VI 190

From *Jeanne d'Arc*, p. 298, "Heroes of the Nations."

Humphrey, Duke of Gloucester . . . 200

From a painting at Strawberry Hill. Ackerman's *History of Oxford*, ii., p. 272. London, 1814.

Seal Appended to the Treaty of Delft, July 3, 1428 208

Photo from original preserved in the archives at Lille. Shield shows arms of Bavaria quartered with those of Hainaut-Holland, placed before the Virgin with the Child. *Legend:* S. Jacob. H'toginne. in Beÿer. gravine. van. Heneg. van Hollant. van Zeelt. v̄a pont. en vrou v̄a vriesl.

Costume in the Time of Henry V. *Tailpiece* 212

From Royal MS., 15 D. 3.

The Countess at an Archery Festival 220

From *Algemeene Geschiedenis des Vaderlands.* J. P Arend, Amsterdam, 1844, ii., 2.

Portrait of Jacqueline 230

Original by Jan Van Eyck has disappeared. Taken from a copy preserved in the Royal Museum at Copenhagen,

Illustrations

	PAGE
No. 180. Wood 2 ft. 4 in. by 1 ft. 4½ in. *Inscription:* "Dame Jacoba de Bavière Comtesse de Hollande." Reproduced from Hubert and Jan Van Eyck. L. Kaemmerer. p. 47 *Kunstler Monographien.* Ed. Knackfuss.	
Portrait of Lord Frank van Borselen .	240
Photo from original at Amsterdam in the Royal Museum.	
Facsimile of Page of MS. Copy of Jean Froissart's *Dittiers Amoureus* . . .	252
Photo from original in the National Library, Paris.	
Humphrey, Duke of Gloucester, and Eleanor his Wife, Received into the Confraternity of St. Albans. 1431	260
From photograph of the original. British Museum, MS. Cott. Nero, D. VII, circa. 1460.	
Statue of Jeanne d'Arc at Compiègne	270
From *Jeanne d'Arc*, by Mrs. Oliphant, "Heroes of the Nations."	
MS. Volume of Froissart	284
Photo from original. 831. National Library, Paris. Phrases on fly-leaves relating to Jacqueline.	
Facsimile of Fly-Leaf with Inscription	306
Facsimile of Fly-Leaf with Inscription	308
Portrait of Jacqueline (*Vrau Jacobe*) .	312
Photo from original at Amsterdam in Royal Museum.	
The Tiger and the Butterfly . *Tailpiece*	314
By kind permission of Anna Botsford Comstock.	

A Mediæval Princess

CHAPTER I

Daughter of Holland

ON St. James's Day, 1401, a little girl was born in the Count's Palace at The Hague, sixteen years after the marriage[1] of her parents, William Count of Ostrevant and Margaret of Burgundy. At the date of his daughter's birth, Count William was Son of Holland, as heir to his father Albert,[2] first Ruward and later Count of Holland, Zealand, and Hainaut. Three years later the child became Daughter of Holland, as acknow-

---

[1] May 11, 1385, *Cartulaire des Comtes de Hainaut,* publié par Léopold Devillers, Bruxelles, 1889, iii., p. x.

[2] The descendants of Albert retained the Bavarian name from his father, Emperor Lewis of Bavaria. Albert's mother, Margaret of Holland, inherited the sovereignty of the provinces in the Netherlands from her childless brother, William, 1346, and left it to her second son, William of Bavaria, whom Albert, the third son, succeeded.

A Mediæval Princess

ledged successor and sole heir to her father, then Count William VI.

Undoubtedly both fatherland and father would have been better pleased with a son. There was some doubt abroad whether the Countship of Holland were not a male fief of the Empire. To be sure this doubt had been settled half a century earlier by the imperial recognition of Margaret as legal heiress to her childless brother Count William IV, in 1346. But the then Emperor, Lewis of Bavaria, was Margaret's husband, and thus he was not disinterested in acknowledging rights that gave honour to his wife and provision for his younger sons. Under other circumstances imperial claims might be revived if the overlord should chance to see personal advantage in a lapsed fief.

The saint on whose day the baby was born was honoured in the name selected, and she was baptised "Jacoba." In Hainaut the name is usually the French "Jacqueline," but it is found in many documents simply as Jacob or Jacque, as Vrouw Jacob, Madame Jacque. In ordinary English litera-

Daughter of Holland

ture she is known as Jacqueline, though she also appears as plain Dame Jake, and often, too, as Jaque de Bavière.

The question of the future husband of this national daughter was an important one and was mooted before she had cut her first teeth. She still lacked some weeks of completing her fifth year when she was formally betrothed to John, Duke of Touraine, second son of Charles VI of France. This alliance was negotiated by the Duke of Burgundy at a moment when he was dominant over the insane king, and it was furthered by his sister Margaret, Countess of Holland, Jacqueline's mother. The betrothal was made an occasion for the grand festivities ever dear to Burgundian princes and was celebrated at Compiègne, whither the Countess conducted the little bride to meet the nine-year-old bridegroom. Nothing was lacking but the presence of the two fathers: Charles was at that moment in one of the crises of his periodic insanity, and a temporary mishap detained Count William, as we learn incidentally from the accounts. To meet the wedding expenses special taxes were imposed, and Philip van Dorp,[1] the treasurer, has left an itemised record of the receipts and expenditures, a record that throws many side-lights on the times.[2] "Item, William and John, Bastards of Holland, Simon van Bruweliis and Gilliis van Gonengiis were sent to the King of France on my dear lord's behalf to tell him that my gracious lord was bitten by a dog and for that reason could not attend the wedding. Allowance for travelling expenses (*teergeld*) 44 French crowns."[3]

Staes, Jan, and Hans, trumpeter, drummer, and piper, are to have six French crowns collectively for their travelling expenses if they will go to the aforesaid wedding.

[1] He was husband to Beatrice, illegitimate daughter of Count William.

[2] See *Codex Diplomaticus Neerlandicus*. Hist. Genootschap te Utrecht, 1853, p. 163. "Rekening van Philips van Dorp," 1406, copied from the original records on parchment in the Royal archives at The Hague.

[3] In another item it appears that the allowance for one messenger with a servant and a horse was one crown per day, twenty-two crowns for twenty-two days. A French crown at this date varied greatly in quality, but it was current at about twenty-five sous tournois, and worth about six shillings. A *livre paresis* was worth a quarter more than a *livre tournois*.

Treasurer van Dorp's receipts in all amounted to about 8600 French crowns, his expenditure was $8210\frac{1}{2}$ French crowns, $25\frac{1}{2}$ groots, and he thus has a clear surplus of $388\frac{1}{3}$ French crowns, $14\frac{1}{2}$ groots. This amount "Philip van Dorp shall include among his assets when he next settles his account."

There was evidently no stinting in the preparations. For instance, even the stay-at-home members of the Count's household were supplied with wedding garments in honour of the occasion, and the single item of trimming for the hats of the councillors was equal to the allowance for a journey to Paris.

There were other doings at Compiègne besides the infant betrothal, as the wedding of Isabella of Orleans was also celebrated, but that is another story and a sad one. The betrothal took place on June 29th, and from that date Jacqueline is designated Duchess of Touraine, although that the ceremony was considered as nothing but a promise for the future, is shown by an article in the contract, that if the bride failed to fulfil her part an indemnity of two hundred thousand golden crowns should be paid to John of Touraine. Another article provided that he should receive a quarter of a million crowns if the birth of a son to Count William should cut off his daughter from the succession. Due provision was also made for Jacqueline's possible widowhood

All formalities concluded, the bridegroom was delivered over to the care of his mother-in-law with an annual allowance of sixteen thousand crowns to provide for his education. Then Countess Margaret and her brother-in-law, John of Bavaria, Bishop elect of Liége, escorted the infant couple to Le Quesnoy, where Count William was awaiting them, probably recovering from his dog-bite, though that is something we hear no more about for the time.

"On Thursday, July 8th, a fine deputation set out from Mons to salute Monseigneur and Madame of Touraine," and it is to be hoped that the children received their "reverences" with all propriety. After this follows a journey to Paris, and then history does not busy herself with recording the

WILLIAM VI, COUNT OF HOLLAND.
XVI century print.

doings of Jacqueline and John, who were being educated for their future responsibilities according to the lights of the time.

On October 23, 1409, Monsieur of Touraine, receives a present of two measures of wine and three fish, the latter significant of feudal duty, while to Madame is given twenty-two ells of cloth of silk, *mout biel*[1] (Hainaut dialect for very fine).

Then in 1412, comes a special dispensation from the Pope to Margaret of Burgundy, permitting her to eat meat on fast days, because she, weakened by her confinement, suffers from a very cold stomach "and, as we hear, fish does not agree with thee." The dispensation is extended to her daughter, the Duchess of Touraine, to the napkin bearer, the cook, and ten other servants who have to test the dishes beforehand."[2] In 1412, several acts are issued in France to the advantage of John of Touraine to suit his requirements as he emerges from the

---

[1] Frans de Potter. *Geschiedenis van Jacoba van Beieren*, p. 21. Mémoires couronnés de l'acad. royale de Belgique, xxxi.

[2] Frans van Mieris. *Groot Charterboek der Graven van Holland*, etc., iv., p. 228 *et al.*

years of childhood.[1] In all these Vrouw Jacob is mentioned as his "wife and dear companion," but the marriage was still in the future. The fact of their consanguinity required a papal dispensation for their alliance, which was granted on May 10, 1411. It is signed by Pope John XXIII.[2]

Four years later the nuptials were celebrated in The Hague with pomp and magnificence.

August 6, 1415, is the date of the first document of public import bearing the joint signatures of the pair recognised as the future rulers of Holland, Zealand, and Hainaut.[3] They pledge themselves to preserve intact the privileges of the land and to follow Count William's example in all things. When the formalities were concluded the young pair departed in state for Hainaut to spend the *white-bread weeks,* as the honeymoon is termed.

---

[1] De Potter, p. 23.
[2] *Groot Placaat Boek,* iii., p. 8. John appears in this as the guardian of his wife. In a way, the provisions imply a recognition of the imperial suzerainty. See Jan Wagenaar. *Vaderlandsche Historie,* xi., p. 400.
[3] Van Mieris, iv., p. 342.

There are many references here and there to the imperiousness of "Vrouw Jacob who early tasted the sweetness of command. So gentle was the nature of the French boy that he meekly obeyed his baby bride during their nursery days, and probably did not abandon the habit when they actually became husband and wife.

Before the year closed the Duchess of Touraine wore a new and prouder title. The death of his eldest brother made John of Touraine Dauphin and heir to the French crown, and the Daughter of Holland became Dauphiness of Vienne. To be sure, the result of the battle of Agincourt had dimmed the brightness of that crown, but there was always hope that under different circumstances its rays would burst through the English mist and shine out with new splendour. Count William showed at this time a far greater preoccupation about his daughter's inheritance than about that of his son-in-law. In the spring of 1416, Emperor Sigismund visited England to further a project of a general European peace. Count

William hastened across the Channel to have an opportunity to see the Emperor and to obtain his promise to recognise Jacqueline as future sovereign in his three provinces. Sigismund was not ready in his acquiescence. Not exactly refusing, he put a counter-question: "Hast thou neither brother nor cousin to be thy heir?" Now Count William certainly had a brother, John of Bavaria, Bishop-elect of Liége. He was a worldly, ambitious, unscrupulous man with great skill in military affairs, wholly unfitted for the ecclesiastical career to which he was pledged. Count William, was rich, too, in cousins free from clerical disqualifications, one of whom might be his heir. But that was not what he wanted. It was his own daughter's rights that he wished to fortify. Apparently he did not attempt to argue the matter with his feudal chief. When repulsed he simply cut short his stay in England, hastened back to Holland, and called an assembly of nobles and cities; and at The Hague on August 15, 1416, "did every noble and each representative of the cities¹ stretch out the fingers of one hand and place the other hand on saints' relics while swearing solemnly, each and all, to recognise Jacqueline as their true sovereign, to aid her against her foes with body and wealth, etc."² Shortly afterwards, the same oath was taken in Hainaut.

It is evident that little heed was paid to feudal obligations. As a matter of fact the bond between Holland and the Empire had long been shadowy.

While Count William was providing for his heir apparent, demands came from France for the Dauphin. The Count was reluctant to trust him in the midst of factions whose leaders showed little regard for any life that might stand in their way Finally he consented that the young pair should meet Queen Isabelle at Senlis while he journeyed to Paris alone.³

Most graciously was the young Dau-

[1] Haarlem, Delft, Leyden, Amsterdam, Gouda, Rotterdam, Oudewater, Hoorn, Schiedam, Alkmaar, Dordrecht, and ten smaller places, besides the cities of Zealand.

[2] Van Mieris, iv., p. 384, etc.

[3] *La Chronique d'Enguerrand de Monstrelet.* (Soc. de l'hist. de France, 1859), iv., chap. 163.

phiness received by the Queen-mother and the nobles. After a few days the Court adjourned to Compiègne, where the childish troth had been plighted eleven years back.[1] This was in Lent, 1417 (1416 o. s.).

In Paris, Count William found things going very ill. Reconciliation between the jarring factions seemed impossible. There was bitter opposition to the Duke of Burgundy, and the Count made his cause his own. "On Tuesday, the next to the last day of March, the Count of Hainaut declared in full assembly of the King's Council that he would put the Dauphin and the Duke of Burgundy in Paris together, or he would take the Dauphin back to Hainaut. A day or two later a rumour came to the Count's ears that there was a plot afoot to capture him and hold him in durance until the Dauphin were restored to his father."[2] "And this was why on the morrow, very

---

[1] The young Dauphin acknowledges a debt of 6000 crowns to Count William, and promises to pay it. This is dated at Compiègne, March 15, 1416 (17). See Van Mieris, iv., p. 365. *Cartulaire des Comtes de Hainaut,* iv., p. 63.

[2] Monstrelet, iv., chap. 163. *Cartulaire,* iv., p. 65.

HÔTEL DE VILLE, COMPIÈGNE.

early in the morning, he pretended to start for Saint-Mor des Fossez, on a pilgrimage, as though he were to return that night to Paris." Once beyond the gates, however, Count William put spurs to his horse and rode with all speed to Compiègne. As he drew near the gate he heard that the Dauphin was ill. When he reached the lad's bedside he found a pitiable sight. Panting for breath, his eyes starting from his head, lay the poor young prince. He was, in fact, already at death's door. On Palm Sunday, April, 1417, he grew steadily worse, on the following day he gave up his gentle spirit and the Easter days that followed had no joy for Jacqueline.

Rumour was busy with the causes of this untoward decease. Some said that, when the Dauphin was overheated from tennis, a servant, bribed by the Armagnacs, had found means to touch his perspiring neck with poisoned hands. Others were ready with tales of other poisoned objects forced into contact with him. All agreed that it was not the judgment of God which doomed the youth to premature death, and Jacqueline to an early widowhood.

Evidently the Count lost no time in leaving Compiègne with his party

"On Easter Monday there set forth from Mons Willaumes de Haucin, etc., with twelve horse and betook themselves to Quesnoy, to our most excellent lord and sovereign and Madame the Dauphiness, to condole with them for the death of Monseigneur the Dauphin."[1]

Six weeks later there was new reason to offer condolence to the young widow. For some time Count William had suffered from a swelling on his thigh, resulting, apparently, from the accident of 1406.[2] When it began to trouble him anew he did not take time to attend to it until after a conference with the Duke of Burgundy at Douay. Then he went to his favourite residence of Bouchain, and called a surgeon to examine the cause of his pain. The sur-

---

[1] *Cartulaire,* iv., p. 67.

[2] See Wagenaar, xi., p. 411. Le Petit states that the wound was an old one, resulting from the bite of a dog. *La grande chronique de Hollande,* i., p. 352.

geon took counsel of none, but proceeded to lance the swelling on his own responsibility. The operation was not successful. It was evidently a case of blood poisoning. The Count grew worse, lost heart, and resigned himself to his approaching end. His one absorbing preoccupation as he lay on his death-bed was the succession of his daughter. The outlook was not promising for her. During two generations Holland had been the prey of certain political factions called the Hooks and the Cods.[1] Count William's adherents were Hooks. The most powerful family in the hostile party was that of the Arkels. Count William had had no more bitter opponent than William of Arkel. Would he be as bitter in his enmity to the daughter? That was a dread that haunted the dying man. Gradually he conceived the notion that if this one foe could be made friend and husband

---

[1] The origin of these names is obscure. The parties came into existence in the contest between Margaret and her son, William of Bavaria. The Bavarian colour, greyish blue, may have led to the comparison of William's followers to codfish, while the term *Hook* was applied to those who tried to catch them.

to Jacqueline, protection would be secured for her and tranquillity for the land. It is said that he proffered the young widow's hand to Arkel, and that his refusal of the honour was a slight never forgiven by Jacqueline. The story does not rest on very reliable authority, though it contains a shadow of probability.[1] Another version is that Count William desired this alliance, but that Jacqueline herself made the proposal, which was rejected. The continuation of Jan van Boendale's *Brabantsche Yeesten*[2] tells another tale:

> "And as the Duke William
> Lay on his death-bed very low,
> So that he never more arose,
> Then he longed and he wished
> That a match should be
> Betwixt Duke John, this is pure truth,
> And his only daughter"

The duke was John of Brabant, son of the Duke Anthony who had met his death at Agincourt. Anthony was a Burgundian,

---

[1] See *Bertha en Jacoba*, J. van Lennep.
[2] Book vii., ch. 55. *Jakobäa von Bayern und ihre Zeit*. Franz v. Löher, i., p. 275, etc. See also *Cartulaire*, iv., p. 70.

brother to Countess Margaret of Holland, and she it was who urged the marriage, as an alliance between her daughter and nephew promised to bring Jacqueline closer in touch with Burgundian interests.

Negotiations to this end were on foot, but nothing was completed when Count William was forced to leave all worldly cares to be settled by others. On May 31st, the Daughter of Holland lost her father, and it was unsupported by husband or betrothed that she turned to her fatherland to ask formal acknowledgment as hereditary sovereign there and in Zealand and Hainaut, after Count William's body had been laid to rest among his ancestors in The Hague. His heart however was carried to Bouchain in accordance with his behest.

CHAPTER II

The Heritage

1417

THERE seemed no lack of natural protectors for the young countess, widowed and orphaned though she were. The danger was lest her protectors might protect too much, because her territories lay in such tempting proximity to their own. On the one side was Jacqueline's paternal uncle, John of Bavaria, bishop-elect of Liége. Only the young niece and his clerical vows stood between him and succession to his brother's land. On the other side was her maternal uncle, John, Duke of Burgundy, who was also Count of Flanders. Brabant, under John, nephew to this duke and to Countess Margaret, was adjacent both to Hainaut and to Holland. The two elder Johns, the Fearless and the Pitiless, had promised the late Count William to protect their niece. This younger John was regarded in the family as the proper husband for the young widow. Geographically nothing could have been better than the proposed union of the lands; nothing more ill matched than the proposed union of the two sovereigns. John numbered fewer years than the sturdy, well-developed, vigorous young woman, besides being her inferior mentally, morally, and physically; but such considerations were ignored in the family conclave.

It was, however, under no other protection than that of her mother that Jacqueline proceeded to take steps to receive homage in her father's lands. In Hainaut there was no delay.

"On June 11th[1] the sheriffs and councillors of the city [Mons] met together, because it was said that Madame the Dauphiness was coming to the city of Mons to take oath of sovereignty, which she did the Sunday morning following."

[1] *Cartulaire*, iv., p. 79.

The province of Hainaut was entirely different from the flats of Holland and Zealand, over which hovered the active genius of commerce. The time spirit of the twelfth century, the spirit of chivalry, with its attendant corps of feudal and mediæval votaries, was dominant among the wooded hills of Hainaut, long after it had disappeared elsewhere before the inroads of modern life. The cities were far behind those of the sister provinces, both in rank and independence. In Mons, the patrician rulers had enforced the ancient law that stray serfs could not be claimed by their masters after the lapse of a year and a day, and had turned many refugees into good citizens, so that the civic population had increased. In Valenciennes, too, there were signs of new burgher life. Still neither place could compare with Ghent, Brussels, or Dordrecht, while a score of lesser Hainaut towns were only beginning to bud into cities, and others remained nothing more than mere castle settlements. As a rule, people and corporations were wholly submissive to nobles and prelates, and of these there was no dearth.

The whole length of the land was about twenty-two leagues, yet that narrow space contained eight counts, one prince, one marquis, six high hereditary officers, and twenty lords lesser in dignity, but entitled to display their own standards or banners.

In addition to these lay nobles, there were those of the Church. Eleven abbots and thirteen abbesses enjoyed the prerogative of wearing great golden crosses on their breasts, and a full dozen were entitled to use crozier and mitre like a bishop. These were live potentates, jealous of the fragments of authority that time and custom had lodged in their hands. There were also dead hands potent in their sway. Where certain saints lay buried was holy ground, offering sanctuary to all that took refuge there for any reason whatsoever; and reason enough there was in those troublous times to cause the immune territory to be well populated.

Jacqueline's progress[1] through Hainaut to

[1] For a description of the progress of a new sovereign, see *Chronica*

exchange oaths of fealty with her subjects of all degrees, followed close on her father's funeral rites. When she and her train arrived before a city, she paused without the gates and waited until a procession composed of priests with their crosses, of city officials of distinguished burghers, and of trade gilds, with banners flying, marched out to greet their new sovereign. If she arrived late in the day and spent the night in a town, she had to leave on the morrow by the same gate which she had entered. As she rode in she was saluted by the ringing of all the bells and by shouts of welcome from the populace. This was her "joyous entry" Flags streamed from the towers, the streets were strewn with flowers, the houses decked with hangings and garlands. Here and there gay-coloured cloths, often embroidered in gold and silver, were stretched across the street. The windows

---

ducum Lotharingiæ et Brabantiæ ac regum Francorum auctore magistro Edmundo de Dynter, lib. vi., Cap. 140, etc. [French translation of De Ram bound in same volume.] Dynter was in the court of John IV of Brabant. See Bibliography; also *Cartulaire*, iv., p. 85; also, Löher, i., p. 291, elaborated with some fantasy.

B   XVᵉ siècle.

were filled with ladies who held chains of flowers which reached over to the opposite houses. Maidens threw wreaths over Jacqueline's arm. Sometimes certain par ticipants who joined in the procession were *personæ non gratæ* to the towns. These were outlaws and exiles who had lurked without the walls, anxiously awaiting the coming of the new ruler, to take the opportunity of returning home under her wing at a moment when feuds were in abeyance, with the hope that she would mediate between them and their judges, so that the ban against them would be removed. At the time of Jacqueline's progress, some of the cities took the precaution of issuing in advance a prohibition against the return of all such undesirable gentry

Once within the walls the procession would advance slowly until it reached the great church. Jacqueline's first action on entering the edifice was to kneel before the holy relics and kiss them. Then, before the high altar, she swore to preserve all privileges and good usages of the city, to protect the Church and the helpless, to strengthen the right and weaken the wrong. There was a whole series of successive oaths in the homage ceremonial.

At Mons, Jacqueline took her first oath upon the relics of St. Waltrude, the town's patron saint; then she took the sovereign's oath in the presence of prelates and nobles at the castle, and lastly she took a third oath to the municipal corporation. Then the procession returned to the church where Jacqueline received homage and renewed or distributed such fiefs as lay in her gift.

In the various localities certain minor customs had to be observed before her investiture was complete into her hereditary rights and her paternal estates, her family property and her sovereign privileges. As a matter of fact, the separation between the two was not very distinct.

Here the ceremonial was terminated by her being led to a belfry where she rang the bell with her own hand. There she went to some cloister or foundation to grant a benefice with hand and brief. Elsewhere, as was the usage in Holland, she appeared before a tribunal, where a trial took place, and she pronounced judgment, and ordered the beadle to execute the same. This was to show that from her emanated authority of the judge, as hers came from the Emperor.

When the actual act of homage was performed, she was seated on a lofty throne, surrounded by hereditary officials. These were nobles in whose families various offices had become mere honorary posts, conferring titles and no duties. Such were the hereditary marshal, cup-bearer, seneschal, chamberlain, and kitchen steward. The day of homage was an occasion for them to appear in the full glory of all their insignia and to go through the form of their titular duties.

The Grand Chancellor and his Privy Council were the first to swear fealty. Then came various executive and administrative officials under a variety of names. These were the Count's own functionaries, wearing his arms and livery like his own household.[1]

---

[1] The immediate household did not have to offer homage. They had taken a new oath on the demise of Count William.

At this time there were fewer hereditary officers than had existed formerly. Sovereigns were beginning to appoint castellans and various other officials for definite terms and at fixed salaries. Gradually a race of modern functionaries were coming into being. It must be remembered that in this early fifteenth century the actual extent of territory administered by the count's deputies was exceedingly small. In all the Church lands the prelates were totally independent. When offering their homage, the clerical dignitaries lent special splendour to the scene with their sparkling staffs, golden crosses, and gorgeous robes, but they were quite conscious that they needed no help from a feudal chief in managing their own temporal as well as spiritual affairs. A few benefices were in the direct gift of the count, and he could ask aid from the incumbents in time of war. That was all.

After the prelates, abbots, abbesses, and capitularies came greater and lesser nobles with their banners and standards. They paid homage, received their fiefs, and swore fealty to their new sovereign as nominal mistress of their estates, but every one remained sole monarch on his own ground.

Nor had the prince any more real concern in the affairs of the cities whose representatives followed the nobles. The civic processions were long and pompous, and the city fathers were proudly conscious of their own importance. At the head marched magistrates and sheriffs, burgomasters and their councils. The patricians followed in a body, surrounded by the gildmasters. Each of these carried a sword, and here and there was one whose gold and silver ornaments showed that he had received the order of knighthood.

The city fathers grouped themselves around the throne and took the oath of allegiance. Then the form of homage was read aloud, and the lifted hands and the acclamations of the assembled burghers were taken as a token of assent to the provisions.

All charters and privileges ever granted to or bought by the cities under Jacqueline's predecessors were confirmed. This was a very important feature in the installation of new rulers on their "joyous entry," and one jealously guarded by the municipal corporations. Their privileges, chartered or customary, were reaffirmed point by point, and the opportunity was taken to point out abuses of the former administration and to demand redress. The homage was, in a way, the occasion of the renewal of a social contract.

When the long series of oaths and pledges was finally completed, festivities of various kinds took place. It was in that wise that the nobles sealed their compact. On their part the cities and the wealthy abbeys offered gifts. A pile of gold pieces on silver salvers was an ordinary civic present. Often, too, it was long before the debts were paid that had been incurred in all haste under the excitement of a joyous occasion.

During the festivities in Mons a frightful hail-storm deluged the city. The sky grew black, and the wind howled. In the neighbourhood the hail killed many cattle and spoiled the chance of harvest. It was considered of ill omen to Jacqueline, who had already met misfortune beyond her years.

Valenciennes was the last town visited. "On Thursday, the 17th of the same month (June), the receivers went from Valenciennes to Mons, because the two ladies were there, who this day, after dinner, departed for Holland."[1]

It was high time that Jacqueline should turn to the northern province. Messenger after messenger had come from the late Count's friends to urge haste. There was by no means as much readiness there to accept the girl sovereign as in Hainaut. The party of the Cods, who had opposed Count William tooth and nail, continued their opposition to his daughter. The fortress of Ysselstein was their headquarters, and within the walls they were prepared to hold out to the last man.

As Jacqueline crossed the frontier, accompanied by many faithful Hainauters, she was met by the most distinguished Hook

[1] *Recette générale de Hainaut*, 1416–17. De Potter, p. 36.

nobles. There was little or no show of pomp and joyousness in city and hamlet. The young Countess made her way soberly to Delft, Leyden, Amsterdam, Haarlem, through the country that looked like a scarred battle-field, and exchanged pledges of mutual protection and good faith with her subjects. She was surrounded by a body of men upon whose personal devotion she could rely, nobles whom she had known from childhood. And none were more devoted to Jacqueline than Eberhard, Lord of Hoogtwoude and Ludwig of Flushing, men who might have felt that her higher position was a grave injustice to them. For these, too, could claim the late Count William as their father. They and their father's daughter Beatrice, now wife of John van Vliet, were all proud to serve their more fortunate sister. And so were two half-brothers of Count William: Adrian, magistrate in Dordrecht, and William of Medemblik.

Jacqueline's uncle of Liége had taken up his temporary abode on an estate of his

PORTAL AT ZUTPHEN.

XV century.

own in Zealand in order to watch affairs in Holland. With his aid and that of Utrecht the defeat of the party in Ysselstein was accomplished, and the rebellious Cod nobles and chief burghers imprisoned. This decisive victory made Jacqueline's progress through the provinces possible.

A very different law of life prevailed in this northern territory. It is true that there was still existent in Holland the scaffolding of a feudal state, but within this frame there had developed a population interested in their own concerns, men in peasant smock as well as in city robes, a farming class and a commercial burgherhood that recognised the prince indeed but no other intermediary lord. The Holland nobles found support neither among peasants nor clergy. Among the country folk old Germanic freedom was not dead. As for the clergy, they counted for little. In Holland neither prelate nor abbot had seats in the Estates. If the prince did not side with the nobles the latter had no support but from their own immediate retainers.

For a time the rich cities had indeed been forced to submit to the nobles' arrogance, but fifty years of comparative peace had given them an opportunity of developing their manufactures and expanding their fisheries. Beukels' invention of salting fish had given an important impetus to commerce. With growth in population, in wealth, and in cultivation came a demand for a part in national affairs. Count William disliked this tendency and checked it, but was unable to suppress it.

The six chief cities were in North Holland. Haarlem was the most important, old and full of rich patricians. In Delft the burghers were somewhat more turbulent in nature In Leyden they were held in check by the hereditary burgrave the Lord of Wassenaar. By the first quarter of the fifteenth century Amsterdam was already rich and populous, rivalling Rotterdam in the south. In Gouda, Cod influence was beginning to be manifest and Oudewater always followed Gouda's lead. All these towns were alive with commercia enterprise. True, the intervening regions were still wooded from stream to stream. From Teylingen to Haarlem there was a stretch of thick forest. But from city to city there were land and water ways, and these were thronged with wagons and boats. There was constant intercommunication, and if the cities chose to unite their forces the nobles were powerless against them. In North Holland, there were various castles of the Hook nobles fortified by towers and moats in the neighbourhood of the cities. Near Haarlem began Kennemerland with its small freehold farms, and in that particular region the nobles did not venture to build their strongholds.

The peasants, fishers, and sailors in Kennemerland were like the Hook nobles in their devotion to the new sovereign. They flocked together to do homage at all the appointed places. On the coast there were Enkhuizen, Hoorn, Medemblik, and Monnikendam, all Hook towns except the first. As yet they were inconsiderable municipalities.

Among the prominent noble families were, first and foremost, the Brederodes, descended from Jacqueline's own ancestors. Then, as an ancient rhyme ran, came the Wassenaars, the oldest, the Egmonts, the richest, and the Arkels, the boldest. But in Holland the power of the nobles at the best paled before that of the burghers, who felt their own independence even in the small corporations.

CHAPTER III

The Second Marriage

1418

THE first acts of the young Countess in Holland were marked by great severity[1] wherever she succeeded in gaining the upper hand. She was, indeed, less harsh than some of her partisan advisers wished, but still executions, scourgings, and other punishments were meted out with no sparing hand to all who had continued their opposition to her father's party. She and her friends felt that radical measures were needful to establish her sovereignty.

But it was only too evident that a girlish, unprotected woman could not maintain her authority. Jacqueline's immediate marriage was eminently desirable and the end of

[1] Her first independent act was permission to Utrecht to destroy the castle of Ysselstein, the stronghold of the Cods, July 14, 1417.—Van Mieris, iv., p. 401.

July found a grand family council assembled at Biervliet to consider the question.[1] The Hook party, the Dowager Countess Margaret, and John of Burgundy all united in urging an alliance between John of Brabant and Jacqueline The Duke sent his son Philip, Count of Charolais, to represent him at the conference. The astute Burgundian perceived at a glance that Brabant would make a fine bulwark against the Empire, if its interests were allied to his. Therefore the very fact that the young pair were singularly ill-mated pleased him, as he also foresaw a probable failure of heirs and a future possibility of all these four provinces passing to collateral heirs, and he was uncle to both Duke and Countess.

Jacqueline's paternal uncle, that "reverend father in Christ," John, Duke in Bavaria, Bishop-elect of Liége, was also present at Biervliet and gave his consent to the projected marriage. Mezeray[2] calls this John

---

[1] Dynter, vi., cap. 142.
[2] *Abrégé chronologique de l'hist. de France,* iii., p. 171. Amsterdam, 1682.

JOHN OF BAVARIA, BISHOP-ELECT OF LIÈGE.
XVI century print.

The Second Marriage

tiger rather than man. John the Pitiless was the title bestowed on him by his con temporaries after a cruel and relentless suppression of a revolt in Liége. Barante is more euphemistic in describing him as a valiant cavalier, devoted to the profession of arms but without real vocation for the Church. His interests were not ignored in the incidental stipulations of the betrothal contract. Whenever he should be pleased to visit his niece, provisions for him and forty attendants with horses were to be furnished free. If he came with a larger escort he would have to provide for the surplus. "This did not please the seigneur of Monjouw, his treasurer, who thought that such a lord should have free access to court, no matter how large was his escort, and that this should be stipulated."[1]

All conditions were discussed at length and finally on August 1, 1417, a marriage contract was signed and the celebration of the nuptials was only postponed until papal dispensation for the union of first cousins

[1] Löher, i., p. 327.

could be obtained.¹ If Duke John failed to fulfil the contract before the following Easter he was to forfeit 500,000 golden crowns. Meantime both were to do everything in their power to obtain the dispensation. All passed off well. The Burgundians had their own reason for being pleased, the bishop-elect showed no opposition and did homage to his niece for his private estates in Zealand, and the family gathering broke up with a fine show of brotherly and cousinly amity, though there was no great prospect of happiness for the bride in the alliance that had been patched up.

Only a few weeks passed, however, and the bishop-elect changed his line of action. He declared that the continued disorders in his father's land were too great to be suppressed without a strong hand and that there was no hand better than his.² He issued a proclamation saying that he had

---

[1] Van Mieris, iv., p. 408, etc.   Jacqueline signed various other deeds on the same day, among which was one making more ample provision for her mother by the donation of many estates.

[2] See a series of Jacqueline's proclamations, etc.—Van Mieris, iv., p. 411 *et seq.*

come from Liége to restore peace and asked to be made ruward or governor in behalf of his niece.[1]

In reply, the Countess convened an assembly of nobles and cities at Schoonhoven, and in their presence declared that she was now of age to manage her own affairs and needed no ruward. She stated her readiness to abide by the Biervliet convention. If her uncle determined to make other claims she would consider them with the advice of her Burgundian uncle and cousin.[2]

The Bishop-elect was present at Schoon hoven when this answer was given. After hearing it he left the assembly, put him self at the head of the Cod party, and accepted the offers of Dordrecht, the one city refusing homage to Jacqueline, to open its gates to him; then he issued letters to the various towns asking their allegiance. Troops were levied on both sides and a pitched battle took place in the neighbourhood of Gorcum early in December. Jacqueline herself rode at the head of her forces,

[1] Dynter, vi., cap. 145.   [2] Löher, i., p. 332.

gave her own orders, and actually scored a victory against her uncle. Among the Cod nobles who lost their lives at Gorcum was Jacqueline's hereditary foe, William of Arkel, who is said by one tradition to have rejected a new offer of marriage made by her on the very eve of this battle. It might have been that she had a desire to escape from an unattractive union, and thought of her father's old dream of uniting the two parties, as a refuge. There is, however, no proof that the incident occurred. Meanwhile preparations for the other wedding went on. After fortifying Gorcum, Jacqueline returned to The Hague to await the results of her embassy to the Pope.

The great council of the Church was just then sitting at Constance. The long schism was at an end, John Huss had suffered the penalty of his heretical utterances, the rival popes were deposed, and Martin V was the accepted head of Christendom. In his hands rested the power to grant a dispensation for the marriage of cousins, and a month after his election the new pope consented to grant the request of the envoys from Brabant. They were men well versed in mediæval methods of persuasion and knew when to disburse the good coin they had carried up the Rhine. Declaring that the relatives of the two young people and the magnates of their lands assured him that the contemplated union would avert frightful wars, Pope Martin V signed and sealed the dispensation[1] on December 22, 1417, and the successful envoys rode triumphantly off to Brabant with all possible speed.

Their haste was necessary. Among the large number of people then present in Constance anxious to further their own ends was the bishop-elect of Liége. Already he had travelled far from the family gathering at Biervliet. Not only was he desirous to set aside his niece's present authority but he was no longer minded to appear in the provinces in the vicarious rôle of guardian while acknowledging his ward as countess in her own right. That right itself he had now determined to dispute, and he had a

[1] *Cartulaire*, iv., p. 109.

powerful friend at his side in the Emperor Sigismund, also present at Constance in 1417.

Now Löher[1] relates that when the Emperor heard of the departure of the Brabant envoys with the dispensation, he hastened to the papal presence and said: "O holy Father, why is the holy council appointed and assembled?"

"My son, so that we may take thought for the interests of holy Church."

"O our Father, that we can not acknowledge."

"Why so, dear son?"

"Why have you half sanctioned heresy by giving permits without the council's concurrence, and thus assisted ill-doing? Brothers' and sisters' children must not unite in wedlock. It is your duty to pardon not to excuse sins."

The words of these reported phrases may be doubted, but there is no doubt that arguments were presented to the Pope in terms strong enough to affect his action. Protests

[1] Löher, i., p. 357.

The Second Marriage

against the proposed dispensation had been, to be sure, already in existence before December 22nd. In September, John of Bavaria had made a formal declaration that the marriage of cousins german was wrong and, in this particular instance, was greatly to the prejudice of the Bishop-elect of Liége. An imperial endorsement of this opinion bears the same date. Thus Martin V certainly need not have rested in the complete ignorance of the other side of the question which he claims for himself. On January 5, 1418,[1] he puts his signature to a revocation declaring in the preamble of the same that he is now better informed and that he has learned that the projected marriage would bring about scandal and bloodshed.[2] Dynter says[3] that this dispensation was allowed to remain unsealed and that the document was invalid long after it had been received in Brabant. There were too many reasons why the marriage suited the Burgundian family for them to allow obstacles to impede the completion

---

[1] Van Mieris, iv., p. 445.
[2] *Non modica scandala etiam diversa homicida.*
[3] vi., cap. 147.

of the matrimonial project which Monstrelet says [1] was the work of Margaret, Jacqueline's mother, and in no wise the desire of the bride.

At the eleventh hour another bridegroom was proposed who might have been much better suited to her taste. This was the second son of Henry IV of England. Out of the united families of Valois and Lancaster, no one was his equal in intellect or had quite as sturdy a character. On March 3, 1418, Henry V gives instructions to William Sturmy and Doctor Richard Leyot to proceed to Holland to offer the hand of his brother John, Duke of Bedford, to Jacqueline.[2] If they were not stayed before they started these gentlemen must have arrived in The Hague just before the celebration of the

[1] Vol. iii., p. 20. There is, of course, no doubt that legal quibbles were employed and that the withdrawal of the dispensation was perfectly well known, but the parties urged a technicality, inasmuch as papers were not sealed and that they did not receive them. "Thereupon neither bull nor authentic *vidimus* was shown to my Lord of Brabant and still less to my Lady of Holland."—*Brabantsche Yeesten*. There are a number of documents signed by Jacqueline during the first ten days of March, evidently preparatory to her marriage (see *Cartulaire*, iv., p. 112 *et passim*).

[2] *Proceedings of the Privy Council of England,* edited by Sir Harris Nicolas, vol. ii., p. 241.

JOHN, DUKE OF BEDFORD, KNEELING BEFORE ST. GEORGE.
Bedford missal. Photo from original.
British Museum, MS. Add., 18850.

other alliance rendered their mission nugatory. The proposal is not referred to in any way by the contemporaneous author who has given the most circumstantial relation of events passing at The Hague at the time.
. In attendance on the envoys sent from Brussels to The Hague in January and February to discuss the preliminary business of the marriage was Master Edmund de Dynter, Duke John's secretary, as the author of the *Brabantsche Yeesten* tells us.[1] He does not himself state that he was actually present at the wedding ceremony, but it may be assumed that he had ample means of information in regard to it. He tells how on Thursday, March 10, 1417, according to French, and 1418, according to Roman style, just at twilight, after vesper service, the Duke and Duchess were married in the palace at The Hague.[2] Master Stephen Wyart,

[1] "*Heeft hertoghe Jan xxiii., der maent janvari Ghesonden heerlijc aan Mier Vrouwen Ingelbrecht greve te Nassauwen, etc. Ende van Dynter meester Emonde Sinen secretaris.*" *Brabantsche Yeesten*, vii., ch. 62.

[2] Dynter, vi., cap. 148. It must be remembered that Dynter was Burgundian to the heart core, and every statement *in re* Jacqueline is a special plea for the righteousness of his patron's proceedings. See also *Cartulaire*, iv., p. 152.

canon from Mons in Hainaut,[1] received the exchange of vows in French. There were present "Dame Margaret of Burgundy, mother of the said Dame Jacque, the noble prince, Monseigneur Adolph, Duke of Mons," besides a host of counts, barons, knights, and noble gentlemen of Brabant, Hainaut, Holland, and Zealand. Moreover, the cities were duly represented by their councillors, and the Duke of Burgundy by the Bishop of Tournay and others. The night following the ceremony was passed by Duke John with the Lady Duchess in the aforesaid castle. Considering the number and rank of the witnesses, it seems extraordinary that "the clandestine nature of this contract"[2] demanded absolution for the contracting parties, but such absolution was given by the vicegerent of the Bishop of Utrecht. Moreover, a second ceremony was performed in church.

"In the same year, and on Sunday, April 10th,[3] the aforesaid duke and duchess con-

[1] The French translator adds "of St. Germain."
[2] *Quare de clandestino contractu.*
[3] *Codex Tegernseer*—the date is different. Posthoc in quarta die

The Second Marriage

tracted and solemnised publicly with appropriate words the said marriage openly in the collegiate church or chapel situated in the said castle, at the hands of the same vicegerent, all due rites being observed. There were present the mother of the said Jacoba, Mme. de Hameide, Mme. de Mont Saint-Martin, Mme. and Mlle. de Lalain, Mme. de Steynkerke, the demoiselle Van den Poele, demoiselle Van den Does, and many more dames and demoiselles, also Monseigneur Willaume Blondel, seigneur of Grevillier, etc., etc.

"It must be noted that there is a chapel in the aforesaid castle at The Hague to which is attached a formal college of secular canons with a deacon as head and canons as members, and from the earliest times one of the beneficiaries of the said chapel has been accustomed to have charge of the souls of the court and of the counts of Holland when resident in The Hague, etc." It was, thus, as the Brabantine secretary emphasises, the

aprilis celebraverunt publice nupcias in facie ecclesie—in ecclesia collegiata ejusdem curie hollandie scilicet—in Hagha comitis hollandie per decanum. etc.

suitable and official place for the marriage ceremony of the "said Duke and Duchess, who are chiefs of their curia and court, and the marriage was solemnised in the said chapel by its dean."

Thus was Jacqueline wedded for the second time. The first rite, performed in March, called *clandestinus contractus,* seems yet to have been so only by a technicality. Certainly a goodly crowd of witnesses were present, and the usual formalities were observed immediately according to custom.[1] Then the second rite in April surely was sufficient to counteract any deficiency in the first ceremony.

With this event John of Bavaria saw the need of his ruwardship vanish. John of Brabant became governor in behalf of his wife. The Bishop-elect had neglected no effort to have the marriage stopped, up to the eleventh hour before its completion. On March 1st the Emperor, still at Constance, wrote as Jacqueline's overlord forbidding the bans.[2] In case the weddin

[1] Dynter, vi., cap. 148.   [2] Ibid., cap. 153.

The Second Marriage

had been celebrated, he ordered an immediate separation of the parties and declared the contract null and void. Then, egged on by the persistent prelate, Sigismund sent an open letter to the cities of Holland, Zealand, and Hainaut, stating that the lands had lapsed lawfully to the empire at the death of Duke William, vassal and companion of the Holy Roman Empire, because he had no male heir.[1] Therefore, he, the Emperor, had bestowed them on John, Count Palatine of the Rhine, Duke in Bavaria, his beloved cousin, for him and his heirs male to hold them of emperor and empire as fief for ever. Now, in spite of this gift, Jacqueline and John of Brabant kept possession of the lands to the injury thereof and against the will of emperor and empire. The Emperor accordingly ordered all officials and all burghers to forsake their obedience to Jacqueline and to accept her uncle as their rightful sovereign.

The Pope, meanwhile, showed an extraordinary readiness to oblige all parties. His

[1] Van Mieris, iv., p. 477.

next step in the proceedings was to grant John of Bavaria dispensation from his half-taken episcopal vows, which enabled him to marry Elizabeth of Gorlitz,[1] an act designed to further the uncle's claims to his niece's heritage. This was at Constance. Once over the Alps and away from imperial influence, Pope Martin changed his tactics and hastened to send to John of Brabant some letters of credence sealed with lead, telling the said Duke of Brabant to give confidence to what two venerable masters in theology, Master Amand de Bremmont and Master Leon de Baest, had to say about the facts of the dispensation. The two venerable masters came into the Duke's presence and showed the papal letters, written on September 5th, declaring that as soon as Martin V was free "from fear of the Emperor"[2] he revoked the revocation wrested from him against his will in January. Duke John might be perfectly satisfied that Jacqueline was his legitimate wife.

[1] She was niece to Sigismund, widow of Anthony of Brabant, an step-mother of John of Brabant.—Dynter, vi., cap. 155.
[2] Dynter, vi., cap. 154. *Sed quam cito Alpes transierit.*

FLOOD IN SOUTH HOLLAND. 1421.
XVIII century print.

The Second Marriage

By the time these reassuring letters reached the court of Brabant, more than a twelve month had elapsed since the ceremonies at The Hague which had defied the papal, imperial, and avuncular orders then in being. Plenty of time if not leisure had been afforded to the bride to repent a precipitate action which had brought her neither happiness nor prosperity.

CHAPTER IV

The Three Johns

AFTER the determined celebration of these nuptials, which he had tried in vain to hinder, John of Bavaria, as already said, had no further excuse for calling himself ruward in behalf of his unprotected niece. She now enjoyed the protection of a husband. But the ex-bishop had no wish to leave his brother's realm in these hands. He changed his line of action. As Count of Holland, Zealand, and Hainaut by virtue of the Emperor's investiture, he proceeded to issue proclamations which he scattered broadcast over the land, offering liberal concessions to all people and cities who would acknowledge him as lawful sovereign lord.[1] He even promised to allow the cities of Holland and

[1] Van Mieris, iv., pp. 477, 478; Van Kampen's *Vaderlandsche Karakterkunde*, p. 173; Bilderdijk, iv., p. 64; Wagenaar, ii., p. 425, *et seq.*; Dynter, vi., cap. 157, etc.

Zealand to convene at their own instance for consideration of common affairs.[1] This is noteworthy as being the first suggestion of such assembly of the States as a regular and legal matter. To Dordrecht he offered several inducements, among which was the establishment of a mint, an especially alluring bait. swallowed eagerly by the city. Dordrecht then became the headquarters of the claimant whom the municipal authorities accepted as authorised by the Emperor. By this time Count John's episcopal pretensions were wholly abandoned. Shortly afterwards, a new bishop was appointed to the see of Liége, Elizabeth of Gorlitz was married to the ex-prince of the Church, and the worthy prelate became secular in outer life.

Jacqueline and John made a formal progress through Hainaut and Brabant, where their coming was duly celebrated. Then they put themselves in battle array to resist their uncle. At first their position seemed

---

[1] Van Mieris, iv., p. 488, date June 20, 1418. Kluit, iv., p. 360. This right of assembly seems never to have been used. Blok, *Geschiedenis van het Nederlandsche Volk*, ii., p 121.

strong. In answer to the imperial candidate's demands for recognition, Hainaut declared roundly that no emperor had any concern with the countship, which was not a male fief anyway, and that female succession had always been allowed.[1] Holland and Zealand said their homage had been duly given to the late Count's heiress, and they wished that the ex-bishop would not put forward such strange novelties.[2]

Jacqueline did not neglect the pen as a weapon, even though seizing the sword. She made a great show as Countess of Holland, and was as lavish in her proclamations as was her uncle. The *Groot Charterboek*[3] preserves many, which were, however, as effective as summons to spirits from the vasty deep. In a growing uncertainty as to which authority would finally prevail, the cities displayed a tendency to disregard the behests of both claimants pending the issue of the struggle.

In Jacqueline's behalf two small armies

[1] May 11, 1418, *Cartulaire*, iv., pp. xvii., 158.
[2] Dynter, vi., cap. 157; Van Mieris, iv., p. 483.
[3] Van Mieris, iv., p. 484, etc.

were collected. At the head of one levied in Brabant, were Duke John and his brother Philip, Count of St. Pol. Jacqueline herself commanded the other, composed of Hainauters, Hollanders, and Zealanders. The two forces marched upon Dordrecht and succeeded in surrounding the city completely. The waterways were cut off or made unnavigable, and blockhouses of heavy wood were built in the neighbourhood to guard all approaches. The defence was, however, equally energetic and effective. After a siege of about six weeks the discouraged Brabanters withdrew, and a little later the Hollanders and Zealanders followed their example, not without loss to themselves. A great part of their baggage fell into the hands of the Dordrechters who overthrew and destroyed the blockhouses erected at Papendrecht.[1]

To Jacqueline's bitter disappointment, the failure of the Brabanters to grant her efficient aid resulted in her definite defeat. Her efforts to hold her ground with her own people proved vain. Rotterdam soon went

[1] Dynter, vi., cap. 162; *Codex Tegernseer,* p. 14.

over to her uncle, and other cities showed every disposition to follow the example.

In October the discouraged Countess was forced to agree to a truce.[1] In December John of Brabant issued a manifesto declaring John of Bavaria heir to Jacqueline if she died without children. By this time Duke John of Burgundy concluded it was needful for him to look after his neighbours' doings, and he again sent his son Philip, Count of Charolais, as his representative, to mediate in the family quarrel. A conference took place at Woudrichem, when both the Johns, Jacqueline, Philip, and a hundred nobles from each party were present, and a treaty was finally signed on February 13, 1419.[2] It was therein stipulated that John of Bavaria should retain what he already possessed—Dordrecht, with South Holland, Rotterdam, Gorcum, and Leerdam, besides the Arkel territories and all that lay between the Lek, the Linge, and the Merwede. All these he was to hold

---

[1] October 27th, Van Mieris, iv., p. 501. This was for eight days. Another was made January 16th to last from January 20th to the following Friday, p. 513.
[2] *Placaat Boek,* iii., p. 9.

in fee simple. In addition, he was to share the government of Holland, Zealand, and Hainaut jointly with John of Brabant for the space of five years. Further, he was acknowledged as heir to Jacqueline.[1] An indemnity of one hundred thousand gold nobles, English mint, was to be paid to him within two years as compensation for his renunciation of the rights conferred by the Emperor. It was thus made plain that he ruled by virtue of the treaty, and the claim of a lapsed fief was abandoned. The fate of the Egmonts was to be decided in consultation with Philip of Burgundy, other exiles were free to return, and all prisoners were to be exchanged without ransom except the senior Arkel.

Various other documents too, were signed at the same time. One by the nobles promised to accept this agreement, and another, by John and Jacqueline, released Dordrecht from all obligations to them.[2]

[1] *Codex Tegernseer*, p. 14; Dynter, vi., cap. 164; Van Mieris, iv., p. 525.
[2] Van Mieris, iv., pp. 525–527. Also *Hist. Genoot. te Utrecht* (1852), p. 117.

By this treaty, says Bilderdijk, John of Bavaria became a hybrid kind of sovereign.[1] He was count in South Holland and joint regent over the remainder of his niece's territory for a stated time. As heir presumptive, his title was Son of Holland, Zealand, and Hainaut.

The astute regent soon found a loophole through which he could crawl from his bare foothold into a little more assured position. As only 15,600 nobles out of the indemnity were paid down, he proposed to release his less clever namesake from further payment and give him, besides, ninety thousand gold crowns if the term of five years were extended to twelve and the regency committed wholly to his charge. Jacqueline's husband accepted this proposition in behalf of his wife's property, and resigned the margravate of Antwerp and the countship of Heerenthals on his own account.

In this second deed there was a special reservation, on the part of the deposed sovereign's husband, that the seal of "our dear

---

[1] *Vaderlandsche Geschiedenis*, iv., p. 70.

and much-loved partner" (*onser liever ende seer beminde gesellinne*)[1] should not be needed to make it valid. It was well to provide beforehand for a refusal which was inevitable. Why should Jacqueline consent to the alienation of her rights?

But this step was not taken until April 21, 1420. Before that Eastertide other events had occurred which affected the Duke and his wife.

[1] Van Mieris, iv., pp. 545, 547. De Potter, p. 60.

CHAPTER V

Domestic Quarrels

THE alliance planned for reasons of state brought no more domestic peace than public tranquillity. It was an unhappy union for both parties. Had John of Brabant been in love with and ready to yield to his energetic and masterful young wife, all might have gone smoothly. He had to be dominated by somebody, and she was quite capable of taking the helm of her husband's one statelet as well as of her own three. But he was probably bored from the beginning by her demands for his aid in her own realm, was wearied with her indignation at his failure to give such aid effectually, and sullen at her exasperation about his high-handed yet cowardly surrender of her ancestral rights to her uncle.

Dominated the young Duke was indeed,

Domestic Quarrels

but by Brabanters, people inimical to Holland interests in general and to Jacqueline in particular. His treasurer, Van der Berg, was especially obnoxious to the sovereign lady and her kin. When this man was murdered in his bed at Mons, dark rumours were whispered about that the Dowager Countess and her daughter were not wholly free from responsibility for the crime, rumours coloured by the fact that the deed was undoubtedly directed by Jacqueline's half-brothers, who, however, had their own personal grudge against Van der Berg. No one knows the whole story, but it is plain that no good came to Jacqueline from this deed of violence, although it freed her from the presence of a foe. For three days her husband bemoaned the loss of his devoted servant and then turned his attention and his affection upon the next person who flattered him. This chanced to be his chamberlain, Everhard T'serclaes. The new favourite ruled his master not only by force of his own will, but also through his young wife, Laurette d'Asche, who bewitched the Duke into giving her the love and devotion never bestowed on his spouse.

John and Jacqueline were indeed a singularly ill-mated couple. From the "white bread weeks" on, there had been rubs between the undisciplined young people, and their many quarrels culminated at Easter, 1420, in a final rupture of the alliance which had been welded with a disregard of obstacles and a persistency worthy of a more brilliant outcome. In the court circles Everhard and Laurette T'serclaes adopted an impertinent tone towards Jacqueline and were imitated by John's other sycophants, who saw that he did not resent disrespect displayed towards his wife. One little insult was heaped upon another. Finally, as a result of the instigation of T'serclaes, John ordered that the whole ducal household should be remodelled. All Jacqueline's ladies and attendants, Hollanders who had been with her from girlhood, were dismissed, and in their stead were appointed Brabant ladies who cared nothing for her and were devoted to the opposing court party. And

JACQUELINE DE BAVIÈRE, 29TH SOVEREIGN OF HOLLAND, ZEALAND, AND
FRIESLAND, COUNTESS AND LADY, TOO, OF HAINAUT.

XVI century print and title.

among them was Laurette T'serclaes. Dynter[1] tells how Jacqueline was at Vilvoorde when this decision was made. Thither rode the Duke and his company. Jacqueline's household were assembled at his order; the ordinance and a list of the new appointments were read aloud and then "Monseigneur the duke mounted and rode off to Fuhr without another word," and without either greeting or taking leave of his wife.

According to the *Brabantsche Yeesten,* just at that time Duke John was very restless, preferring, perhaps, to be anywhere rather than in the company of his injured wife. Sometimes he hunted in the forest of Soignies, occasionally he went over the Senne, sometimes he stayed awhile at Fuhr, now he was at Vilvoorde, now he betook himself to Antwerp. When Jacqueline was informed of the publication of the list she gave hasty orders which were promptly fulfilled, and flinging herself on her saddle, she galloped after her lord, followed by a single gentleman and three demoiselles. As soon as she

---
[1] vi., cap. 167. See also *Brabantsche Yeesten,* vii., ch. 80.

arrived in her husband's presence, weeping great tears, she asked why he wanted to send away her ladies of high degree and noble blood, ladies of good life and reputation, wise, honest, and in all respects worthy dames, and, for the most part, educated with her from childhood.

Her voice rose higher and higher as she proceeded to reiterate the fact that she had been no undowered bride but an independent heiress, and it was her right to maintain the state to which she was accustomed before her marriage.

Untouched by this outburst, John replied that he had his own reasons for changing the household and he had taken care to give his wife noble and worthy demoiselles of Brabant as attendants. More and more enraged at his assumption, Jacqueline declared again that she did not care how noble the new ladies were. Her Holland dames, too, were noble, and, in addition, they were her friends from infancy, and them she would have. But neither arguments nor passion nor invective availed. The ducal household was arranged nominally according to the list, but, in spite of orders, Jacqueline persisted in retaining certain of her most valued friends, though all their posts were filled by other appointments and the salaries were paid to the new incumbents.

"From this moment conjugal love began to weaken and grow chill day by day until it was totally extinguished and forgotten, as will appear later," says Dynter.

It is, after all, a tale of the pettiest kind of domestic bickering, at least as it is related by chroniclers and poets. The atmosphere was thickly clouded in the early spring of 1420 and relations were strained. The court was then at Brussels.[1] The custom there was for the courtiers to assemble at two formal meals daily, while bread, wine, and light refreshments were served in their private apartments in the early morning and in the evening. Now, when it became apparent that Jacqueline was determined to retain her Holland favourites in spite of ducal behests, T'serclaes resolved not only

[1] Dynter, vi., cap. 167.

to make it unpleasant for them, which he and his friends were doing diligently, but, as insults attained no result, further to resort to the petty expedient of starving the ladies out.

The refreshments sent to the Hollanders' rooms became more and more scanty until the supply ceased entirely. All that the ladies consumed outside of the dining-room they were obliged to provide for themselves. Complaints helped nothing and soon T'serclaes pushed matters to still greater extremity. On Easter, April 7, 1420, there was a great festal dinner. The chamberlain ordered the servants to ignore the Holland ladies as though they were not seated at the table. The orders were strictly obeyed. While the whole court of Brabant feasted gaily on Easter delicacies, while Jacqueline and her Brabant dames were served with the best, the Holland ladies sat hungry before empty plates and were the laughing-stock of the remaining guests, until they left the banquet in tears. It happened at this time that the Dowager Margaret came to Brussels and stayed at an inn, the Mirror, in the rue de la Montagne. Naturally this scandal was reported to her. Straightway she hastened to the palace to upbraid her son-in-law. Her angry reproaches did not move him. She left the palace and returned to her hostelry, whither her daughter followed her. No carriage was at the service of the Duchess of Brabant. It was on foot, weeping, attended by one faithful servant, Jan Rasoir, that the miserable Jacqueline sought her mother's inn. On the following morning the two ladies shook off the dust of Brabant and went to Hainaut, the only one of her provinces on whose faithfulness the poor, despised Countess of Holland, the neglected wife of the Duke of Brabant, could still count.[1]

Coincident with the course of this court and family scandal, ran the further negotiations between the ex-bishop of Liége and John of Brabant, which resulted in the cession to her uncle of Jacqueline's sovereignty over her territories for the space of twelve years. This last and most injurious treaty[2]

---

[1] Dynter, vi., cap. 172.   [2] Van Mieris, iv., p. 545.

bears the date of April 21, 1420, a few days after Easter. As mentioned before, among the articles was one expressly providing that the stipulated conditions should be fulfilled, and "our dear uncle" should not be disappointed even if the seal of the Duchess of Brabant failed to appear on the parchment.

That is not all. The time appointed for the fulfilment of the compact was St. James's Day of the current year, and another pledge was given by John of Brabant in regard to it. The uncle was evidently a little sceptical as to the consent of his niece to the nefarious transaction, and took pains to assure some compensation for himself in case he were deprived of the security of her formal consent to being deposed. In a document of April 22nd, John promises to pay his uncle 26,000 crowns, if Jacqueline's signature were not obtained before July 25th.[1] Some of Jacqueline's biographers consider that this date, her own birthday, was an added insult to the proposed alienation of her count-

[1] Van Mieris, iv., p. 547. De Potter, p. 61.

ships—a piece of fantasy that may go for what it be worth. Without any refinement of cruelty there had certainly been sufficient cause to justify Jacqueline in her revolt against marital authority when she fled away to Hainaut.

CHAPTER VI

Refuge in Hainaut

THE cities of Hainaut, especially Mons and Valenciennes, possess carefully kept records of their expenditures, and out of these items much information can be culled respecting Jacqueline's movements and her ways of life, especially during the months that followed her departure from Brabant, a period that she spent in company with her mother in her various castles. There is much, too, to indicate how closely her earlier life was identified with Hainaut.

Just before her marriage she founded a little chapel at Bouchain, where a daily mass was celebrated for the repose of her father's soul.[1] This was in February, 1418, the same month when other records show her care to endow her mother with such estates as lay

---
[1] Van Mieris, iv., p. 459. *Cartulaire,* iv., p. 114.

in her gift, several within the Hainaut territory. In Jacqueline's case the usual routine of anti-nuptial settlements had been reversed, the bride being donor instead of recipient.

But it was not only in token of filial respect that Jacqueline made gifts whose records appear in the account books. She was evidently generous. We find traces of many presents, great and small, bestowed right and left. Here a pension is given to minstrels who had brought "much content to my Lady of Hainaut"; there, four priests of Quesnoy and the school-master, "who sing vespers and masses in the dwelling of my Lady," are invited to sup after vespers and to dine on the morrow. The Burgundian historian makes her defy her husband for the sake of her Holland court ladies, and there are many proofs of her care for her humbler attendants. Remembering all the agreeable services performed for her by Agnes Poulette, her foster-sister, she renders her marriage to Pierart Willesme easier by the settlement of a pension of sixty-five pounds tournois. This was to fall due on April 1st, and the receipts of the annual payments are duly chronicled.[1]

There were christenings as well as weddings, which she honoured with her gifts. An infant, Marie de Harpre, receives from her a bowl of white silver costing seven pounds ten shillings, and the godmother does not forget nurse and priests.

To mention all her beneficiaries would fill many pages. It is only worth noting how often some adjective has crept into the dry entry, which shows the giver's personal interest in her protégés.

The accounts of this year also suggest little pictures of her surroundings. Evidently the castle of Quesnoy was furbished up. One Jehan, a Florentine, living at Valenciennes, cleans the Duchess's white chamber, "the one that is hung with tapestry wrought with peacocks, and with figures of maidens playing on the harp." The tapestry was in a bad condition and had to be relined with Burgundy cloth. In addition,

[1] De Potter, p. 81 *et seq.*

Jehan cleaned another chamber and a green room, one hung with hunting scenes, and the other with representations of the battle of Jerusalem.

Evident it is that Jacqueline had a taste for pomp and luxury. In the last journey made with her husband, just before that fatal Easter, their whole expenses at Mons, March 18th–26th, amounted to £854 11s. 8d. Her own household consisted of a long retinue of attendants, among whom we find mentioned a guardian of " the white dogs." This was an office of great consideration, apparently, for its incumbent received a salary of two hundred pounds, a good income in comparison to the thirty pounds of a private secretary.

Jacqueline did not retire to private life after she had thrown off marital authority. The traditional nine points of the law were in her uncle's favour in the north, and her armed invasion of Holland accomplished nothing in dislodging him. In the south, however, she was in possession, and as sovereign Countess she convened the Estates of Hainaut in July. The first act of the deputies was to send envoys to Brabant to try to effect a reconciliation between the divided pair. The Duke's statement was emphatic: "Nothing in the world do I desire more than the return of my wife to my roof." It was, however, the last thing that Jacqueline desired or intended, and so she roundly declared. Other negotiations followed respecting her dower right, her maintenance, etc., and the months passed by without the breach being healed.

In Brabant affairs were in a very bad way. Brussels arose in open rebellion against her Duke's authority, and finally came out best in the struggle. The Estates were divided against themselves, and the distrust of the Duke's capacity was so great that his brother, the Count of St. Pol, was appointed ruward for the time being. It was not until the early months of 1421 that John was again master in Brabant. This was after Jacqueline and her mother had appeared in person before the Brabant Estates to urge their own claim. But all that is another story, and belongs to the heritage of the Duke, not to the flight of the Duchess.

Jacqueline at last determined to take her affairs completely into her own hands. She declared that her conscience had always been uneasy about the legality of her marriage, and now she was convinced that it had not been crowned by the blessing of Heaven. Never had she seen John of Brabant cross the threshold of her room without trembling like an aspen leaf, fearing that she was committing mortal sin. So she declared, and so, perhaps, she believed, after the same John had alienated her paternal heritage, deprived her of the companions of her youth, and treated her with personal indignity. She called wise men into her counsel and laid the matter before them. They needed no occult power to interpret the bias of her wishes; and while they did not actually consent to the proposition that the marriage was null and void, they also failed to assert its unquestioned validity. Jacqueline found no difficulty in having her brief made out in due form to lay before the Estates of Hainaut when they convened February 19, 1421. The gist of her statement was simple, and showed four reasons why the union between Duke and Countess was invalid:

1. They were the children of a brother and sister, thus cousins in the first degree.

2. Jacqueline's first husband, John of Touraine, was a blood relation of John of Brabant.

3. The Dowager Countess Margaret was godmother to John of Brabant, and thus he and Jacqueline were spiritual brother and sister.

4. At the moment when they were united in marriage the force of the first papal dispensation was annulled by the papal revocation.

Jacqueline prayed that the Estates should have the matter investigated anew, and declared that her conscience forbade her return to her husband without a new papal dispensation.

The Estates did not know what to do. Their first step was to despatch an embassy composed of nobles, citizens, and clergy to

Duke John, to inform him of his wife's suit, and another to Philip, now Duke of Burgundy, as he had succeeded his father, John, after the latter's murder by the Dauphin on the bridge at Montereau, in 1419. Young, ambitious, domineering, Philip was quite determined to gain control over as much of the world that was before him as possible, and was vitally interested in all that went on in his cousin's domains.

"On Sunday, March 2nd, there departed from Mons, Jaquemars Baudon, sheriff with escort and with certain gentlemen from among the prelates and nobles to Monseigneur of Burgundy, whom they found at Ghent," to inform him "respecting the difference between our very excellent lord and lady of Brabant on account of their marriage. The said Monseigneur of Burgundy gave a very gracious and courteous response, saying that on a certain day he would be at Brussels, and they might send envoys to him there about this matter."[1]

Philip's intervention was something that

[1] De Potter, p. 88.

Jacqueline was afraid of. Rumours came to her ear that her powerful cousin would not leave Brussels until he held in his hand a net to entrap Brabant and Hainaut, just as her other kinsman had acquired Holland and Zealand. It might be his intention to snare her too within that same net under the guise of personal protection

This time Jacqueline determined that no one, not even her mother, should select a protecting guardian for her. She was allied to other princes besides those of the House of Burgundy and Holland. Through Philippa of Hainaut,[1] Henry of Lancaster was also her kinsman, and to him she now decided to appeal.

Chastellain tells in pretty, though perhaps imaginative language, how one Robessart, seigneur of Escaillon, English at heart, filled his lady with enthusiasm for England, where he had spent much time. There she would find gallant gentlemen ready to espouse the just cause of an oppressed dame.[2] Wher

[1] She is the Queen for whom Queen's College, Oxford, was named
[2] *Chronique*, i., chap. 71. See also Monstrelet, iv., livre i., chap. 236.

HENRY V.

she finally told him, of her own accord, that she was resolved to seek refuge in the court of Henry V, "he was not at all angry, but very joyous,"[1] and at once thought out ways and means of preparing for this adventurous departure. She already had in her possession a passport signed by Henry V, permitting her and the Dowager Margaret to pass through the English lines in France on their way to Ponthieu, where she possessed some dower estates. That would give her entry into Calais.[2] In this document only Jacqueline's hereditary titles are used. There is no mention of the "Duchess of Brabant," a name she had resolved to discard for ever.

There may have been some rumour afloat of Philip's immediate designs against her personal liberty that led Jacqueline to hasty and secret flight.

One of the last acts of the Countess in "our city of Valenciennes" in 1421 was to order "our dear and loyal councillor Guillaume du Cambge," receiver of Hainaut, "to

---

[1] *Il n'était pas courroucé mais très joyeux.*
[2] See Rymer's *Fœdera*, x., p. 67.

give our dear varlet, our harper Jehan, in recompense for the agreeable services he has rendered us, the sum of 12 crowns in gold, to enable him to make a journey to St. James in Galicia."[1] Could this pilgrimage have had the real end of obtaining good auspices for the harper's mistress in her new enterprise? Perhaps. St. James was her own patron. A few days later and Jacqueline took leave of the Dowager for a short visit to Bouchain, praying her to be content that "she abandoned her for a night or two. On the morrow or the third day at the latest" she would return without fail to her mother.[2] Once out of the gates of Valenciennes, she met Escaillon with sixty horse; under this escort she rode at the top of her speed toward Calais. One night they spent on the way. Rising very early on the morrow they journeyed on to Calais, where the lady and her suite were most honourably received the English officers evidently having been forewarned of the coming of the fugitive.

[1] *Bulletin de la Commission royale d'histoire*, 2ᵉ série, vii., 352. Also De Potter, p. 84.
[2] Chastellain, i., p. 214.

At Calais she waited while a messenger crossed the Channel to ask the English king his pleasure. During his short absence, Jacqueline mounted often on the walls of the fortifications and strained her eyes to see whether her envoys were yet in sight. "She could just discern," says Chastellain, "the white cliffs of England" At last she spies a sail set to the wind, and within the bark sit the messenger, Gerard de Poelgeest, and his two comrades. Gerard was a Hollander, a faithful Hook, and devoted to his dispossessed sovereign.

It was a hospitable message of proffered welcome sent back by Henry V, and Jacqueline did not delay in accepting the invitation, or rather gracious permission, to make England her home till her fortunes mended. She set out at once on "a journey neither profitable nor worthy either for the lady or her adviser Escaillon. As you will think," adds Chastellain, "when you know what a dire and mortal war resulted by which she was expelled from her heritage and exposed to the hardship of a contrary fortune nearly all the course of her life." Her fortunes could hardly have been more contrary than at the moment when she crossed the Channel, and it was full of hopes that the tide might turn that she sailed to the white cliffs and found the King's brother, Humphrey, Duke of Gloucester, "who had never yet wedded a wife," waiting at Dover to escort her to his brother's court. Jacqueline mounted the palfrey thoughtfully provided by Humphrey, and they set off for London, which they reached at an early hour on the following day. "Humphrey conducted her to the King, who received her most graciously, and paid her such honour and favour as befitted a grand princess, former dauphiness of Vienne, and one who might have been Queen of France."[1]

After the insults of the Brussels court it must have been pleasant to come to a place where her past dignities were remembered. Probably Henry V, with his continental ambitions, also took into consideration the value of his guest's hereditary lands as a

[1] Chastellain, i., p. 217.

bulwark to the English in France. As an international balance of power the Countess of Holland and Hainaut might be a convenient ally. So for the present moment the prudent king was glad not only to recognise her kinship, but to provide for her immediate needs, in the hope of future rewards for his hospitality

CHAPTER VII

Jacqueline in England

1421-1424

"ON Saturday March 8th, came tidings to Mons at about dinner time that our very excellent Lady had departed from Valenciennes on the previous Thursday and had gone to sleep at Bouchain and on the morrow had departed thence to go, so they say, to Calais, and that she was there on Saturday March 8th."[1]

Thus reads the record of the flight of the Duchess as it stands in the register of her ancient capital. One biographer, Cocqueau, writes[2] that Jacqueline's intention to flee to England appears "from the letter of Margaret her mother advising messieurs that

[1] *Premier régistre des consaux de Mons. Cartulaire*, iv., p. 271.
[2] *Beiträge*, p. 46. Cocqueau finished his *Chronique de Valenciennes* in 1578, having had access in Hainaut to many records which are now lost.

Jacqueline in England

her daughter had departed on March vi to go to some destination which she would announce later—by the letter of the Duke of Burgundy saying he had heard of the said departure, and would give his aid to the Duke of Brabant in regard to it, and would discuss matters with his aunt,—from the fact that the Duke [of Brabant] sent deputies to Valenciennes to consider this affair, and to command them to retain the possessions of his wife which she had sent for from England—and from the requests of her mother begging protection—and from Jacqueline herself, writing from Calais, ordering her property to be forwarded to her "

It was the Dowager Margaret who had to meet the dukes of Burgundy and Brabant and the corporations of Jacqueline's towns to discuss with them this last action of her headstrong daughter. She could do little but show "certain letters" declaring in no uncertain terms that Jacqueline was fully determined never to return to "the obedience of John of Brabant." Moreover, rumours that the English king's brother, Humphrey of

Gloucester, was the magnet attracting the Countess to England were soon current in Brabant, in Holland, and in Flanders. There is no actual record that the two had ever seen each other before Jacqueline's arrival in Dover. Yet the fact of a previous meeting is quite possible. Humphrey took a part in public affairs from the time of his leaving Oxford, and went abroad from time to time on errands of diplomacy, of ceremony, or of war. He it was who rode his horse into the water to greet the Emperor when he visited England in 1416, and to receive assurance, before he set foot on English soil, that he cherished no ulterior purpose of imperial suzerainty over the island. As an extra courtesy Gloucester, too, speeded this parting guest by escorting him as far as Dordrecht. On his own return journey the Duke may have paused to pay his respects to the Count of Holland. The latter had recently left England in some dudgeon, but his quarrel was not with the King, and not long afterwards the Duke of Bedford was proposed as Jacqueline's husband.

THE POET LYDGATE IN HIS STUDY.
British Museum M. Harleian, 2248.
XV century.

Jacqueline in England

When Jacqueline's reception at the English court was reported abroad, messengers were speedily despatched from the two Johns and from Philip of Burgundy to Henry V, demanding the return of the fugitive. The Duke of Burgundy was especially furious at this event, and there were several reasons for his anger. Humphrey had been a candidate for the hand of Philip's sister, Anne of Burgundy, and the suggestion that he was turning his thoughts to another bride and one whose divorce was simply pending, not decided, was an insult to the Burgundian family. Moreover, Philip was fully intending to be heir to all his kinsfolk in Holland, in Hainaut, and in Brabant. At this epoch John of Bavaria was undoubtedly *de facto* sovereign count in Holland and Zealand; but it must be remembered that his style was still Ruward in behalf of his niece, and Son of Holland as her heir presumptive. But he himself had no heir, and in the eyes of his cousin of Burgundy he was, like John of Brabant, merely a temporary incumbent of Philip's own future territories. A new question would arise, however, if the real heiress were to take a new husband, whose possible descendants might prove a block in Philip's progress towards her portion of the fair heritage adjacent to his present lands. Moreover, the Duke was an ally of England, an alliance that suited him more than passing well, and he did not wish to be forced to break it on account of a foolish escapade of his cousin of Hainaut and because of her plaints about her father's lands, which were very well off under the guidance of her uncle and heir.

Perhaps it was Philip's vehement protest that led Henry V to keep Humphrey and Jacqueline apart for a time until their path was smoothed a bit. At any rate, Jacqueline had been in England but a few weeks when the Duke of Gloucester was ordered to France, where there was plenty of work awaiting the English, if they were to make good the claims of Henry V to be heir to his father-in-law, Charles VI, in lieu of the latter's son, who had been formally disinherited by the Treaty of Troyes, 1420. The

Dauphin's party had no idea of accepting his disinheritance, and were fighting the English troops with all the forces that could be collected, while the invaders were sparing neither money nor blood. Among the slain at the battle of Baugé in the spring of 1421 was the Duke of Clarence, third son to Henry IV. At the time of Jacqueline's arrival in England, Henry V was straining every nerve to prepare for a campaign in France which should avenge his brother's death and strengthen his own position— untenable, in truth, on any ground of equity.

May 27th is the date of Duke Humphrey's passport, and probably also that of his leaving England. Two weeks later Henry followed him across the channel.

On June 10th, the very day of his own departure, the King executed several acts. One,[1] "in behalf of the Countess of Hainaut," provided for the release of John Bloun

---

[1] Rymer, *Fœdera*, x., p. 129. Henry made other personal preparations at Dover just before setting sail, as the codicil to his will shows: "I have made this Will be myself and writen hit in hast with myen owen hand, thus enterlynet and blotted as hit is, the IX day of June ye yere of oure Lord MCCCCXXI and of my regne ye IX." See also *Proceedings of Privy Council*, etc., iii., p. x.

dell, knight of Hainaut, prisoner in the Tower of London. This is issued at Dover by the King himself.[1] Nor did Henry's kindness toward his guest cease with his absence. Jacqueline remained in England with Henry's queen, a sister-in-law of her own infant marriage—that Catherine of France whose wooing by the English King is so charmingly suggested by Shakespeare. Perhaps it was her intercession that procured the next favour for her guest, granted by Henry's order, which is recorded in Rymer.[2] It is a provision of £100 a month for *Dame Jake Duchesse de Holand* so long as she sojourns in England. This was to be taken from the revenues of Joan, late Queen of England. The document is dated at Westminster and given under the royal seal, though of course in the King's absence.

The sum is very liberal for the time. It was certainly needed by Jacqueline, as her desired property had not been sent after her according to her request. Of returning she

---

[1] *Gesta Henrici Quinti*, p. 153. *Apud Dovorriam, per ipsum Regem.*
[2] Rymer, x., p. 134. See also order in Council, July 8th. *Proceedings and Ordinances of the Privy Council*, ii., p. 291.

had no thought. Nor did she recognise a marital tie as existing any longer between her and John of Brabant. At her orders, declarations that the marriage was null and void had been posted on the doors of the chief churches in Hainaut and in Holland. Undoubtedly the great inducement to England to further Jacqueline's alliance with the King's brother was the hope of annexing her domains to the other continental acquisitions of the royal family. Her affairs were made a matter of national importance. And such they became, for she promised to give Humphrey her lands as a marriage gift, *conthoralem*.[1]

This was a point that aroused Philip's righteous indignation. "What! should a woman be allowed to alienate her realm from her own kin? Nay, it behooved her natural guardians to prevent such a step."

In December, at Windsor, was born the sixth Henry, the Englishman who was to ally the title of King of France to that of England, according to the promise wrung

[1] *Gesta Henrice Quinti*, p. 154.

from the insane French monarch by Henry of Lancaster.

"And about this time word came to the king through trusty messengers of the birth of his son Henry VI whom the queen had borne on the feast of St. Nicholas in England at Windsor."

"And his name was given him Henry," says Stow, "for there received him at the font John, Duke of Bedford his uncle Lord Warden of England and Henry the king's uncle, Bishop of Winchester, and Jaquelyn Duchesse of Holland that remained then in England."[1] Thus Jacqueline was honoured by an invitation to hold the baby prince at the font, the baby whose royalty was destined to be of as little advantage to him as were her many titles to his godmother.

Meanwhile the Duke of Burgundy steadfastly refused to acknowledge the slightest legality in the writs of divorce that Jacqueline had had affixed to the church doors. Duchess of Brabant she was and Duchess she should remain. In the face of his oppo-

[1] *Chronicle*, p. 361.

HENRY V AND CATHERINE OF FRANCE.

sition, Henry V continued firm in his refusal to allow any marriage with his brother to take place. But Fate removed him from the scene The France which he was hoping to make a British province furnished a death-bed to the ambitious, energetic warrior king. In August, 1422, an illness seized him, and he succumbed to it in the woods of Vincennes, leaving his nine-months-old son as heir to both realms. At that moment Humphrey of Gloucester was warden of England, as the Duke of Bedford had escorted Queen Catherine over to France to see her husband. The guardianship of the King's person and the regency of the two kingdoms were henceforth divided between Bedford, Gloucester, and their uncle of Winchester, the exact division of responsibility and of powers varying with circum stances.[1] Humphrey, left for the moment to his own devices, determined to consider Jacqueline as duly freed from her obnoxious marriage-bond by virtue of the public notices. There is a tradition, which Wagenaar

---

[1] *Proceedings of the Privy Council,* vol. iii., *et passim.*

does not hesitate to adopt, that, weary of receiving no decisive answer from Martin V, Jacqueline turned for aid to the anti-Pope, Benedict XIII (Pedro da Luna), acknowledged by no country but Spain, and from him obtained a formal nullification of the Brabant marriage[1] No contemporary author mentions this statement and there is little probability of its truth. As neither England nor Hainaut recognised the claims of this Pope, it is hardly probable that any one would venture to urge the validity of his word over and above the authority of Martin V, whom they did recognise. Dynter says: "The Duchess Jacqueline made a matrimonial alliance *de facto* with the illustrious prince Lord Humphrey, the Duke of Gloucester, the brother of the English king, without waiting for the judgment of the Church, whence arose many inconveniences."[2] The exact date of the celebration

---

[1] *Beiträge*, p. 49; De Potter, p. 96; Wagenaar, iii., p. 453.

[2] vi., cap. 192: "*judicio ecclesie non expectato—unde multa inconveniencia.*" Dynter also says, "*sine medio ecclesiæ.*" In the records of the Paris trial it is stated "*contraxerunt ad invicem matrimonium secundum morem ecclesiæ.*" *Beiträge*, p. 50.

In the *Tegernseer* MS. there is a statement that the nuptials were

of the marriage does not appear. Jacqueline writes to the Estates of Hainaut from *Hardfort en Engleterre,* ordering them to convene on September 26, 1422.[1] There is no mention here of a new title for her, nor is there in the warrant for the payment of £100 to the Duchess of Holland, December 20th of the same year (1422). That the news of her alliance first leaked out instead of being formally announced may be inferred from the tale told in the minutes of the council sitting at Mons in October, 1422:

"On Sunday 25 day of October, 1422, returned from the city of Hal before dinner Simons li Douls, Gilles Poulés sheriffs [and others][2] and this day after dinner was the council assembled in the government house. There were present 36 persons. In the presence of the above was related by the mouth of Andriu Puche all that had passed with M.

celebrated regally in England without the consent of King Henry. *Quibus nupciis regaliter in anglia celebratis licet fuit præter consensum heinrici regis anglie.* Beiträge, p. 16.

[1] *Cartulaire,* iv., p. 310; *Minutes of Council, Proceedings,* etc., p. 11.

[2] Here follow the names of the deputies from the various places. *Cartulaire,* etc., iv., p. 317.

of Brabant and his council at the meeting at Valenciennes on the affairs already noted, etc. . . . There was also speech of the news come to Monsieur of Brabant that our very redoubtable lady was remarried to the Duke of Gloucester, brother of the King of England, lately dead and of the report that the said lady is already *enchainte de vif enfant* and wishes to come to Quesnoy for her confinement and expects 6000 archers to accompany her."

In a petition presented to Humphrey by Jacqueline's old friend, Robessart, on March 7, 1423, he is addressed as "*Duc de Gloucestre, Comte de Hanau, Hollande, and Zeellande,* etc."[1]

In February, however, the rumour became certainty in Hainaut. On Tuesday, February 9th, the three Estates were ordered to assemble, "because on Thursday Feb. 11th our very revered hereditary lady wished that announcement should be made of the state of marriage of her, our said lady, with the Duke of Gloucester."[2]

[1] Rymer's *Fœdera*, x., p. 279.   [2] *Cartulaire,* etc., iv., p. 328.

Jacqueline in England

Duke Humphrey of Gloucester is a picturesque figure in the various places where he crosses the pages of history and fiction. He was markedly less able than John, Duke of Bedford, the former pretendant for Jacqueline's hand. The two brothers, indeed, seem to have developed the different sides of their father's character.[1] Humphrey has the adventurous spirit, the popular manner, and ambition; John has all the seriousness, the statesmanship, the steady purpose, the high sense of public duty that in a lower degree belonged to his father. Bedford, again, has all the great qualities of Henry V without his brilliancy; Gloucester has all his popular characteristics without any of his greatness. The former was thoroughly trusted by Henry V: the latter was trusted only so far as it was necessary.

Humphrey had a keen interest in the learning of the day, and was early known as the patron of letters. The poet Lydgate says·

"Duc of Gloucester men this prince call;
And notwithstanding his state and dignite,

[1] Stubbs, *Constitutional History*, iii., p. 97.

> His corage never doth appalle
> To studie in books of antiquite;
> Therein he hath so great felicite
> Vertuously himself to occupie,
> Of vinous slouth to have the maistrie."

He it was who "magnified" the University of Oxford "with a thousand pounds worth and more of precious bokes." There were one hundred and twenty-nine volumes in the gift sent by Humphrey to the new library over the Divinity School, whose building he aided, and which still bears the name of Duke Humphrey's Library. A letter was despatched to the House of Commons asking them "to considere the gloriose gift of the graciose prince—to thanke hym hertetyly and also prey Godde to thank hym in tyme coming when goode dedys ben rewarded."[1] Some manuscripts once possessed by him are also to be found in Paris. The motto placed in his books was *Moun bien mondaine*. "Hearne in his esteem for this religious, good and learned Prince quaintly says that he used, whenever he

---

[1] *Annals of the Bodleian Library*, W. D. Macray, p. 6.

saw his handwriting in the Bodleian Library,[1] to show a particular sort of respect for it."

Humphrey's connection with the Oxford library was, however, some years later than his alliance with Jacqueline. In the years of his regency his whole attention was demanded by other than literary matters. At home there were the affairs of the minor king, while Jacqueline's heritage was a tempting bait enticing him to the continent. The idea of acquiring an independent realm for himself was, naturally, attractive to the cadet of a royal house, even though he had shown all zeal in serving the interests of his brother and nephew.

In spite of the irregular character of the divorce Jacqueline was acknowledged as Duchess of Gloucester without question in England and received as a member of the royal family

In the abbey of St. Albans was a certain unknown monk who from 1420 to 1431 jotted down daily memoranda on various events which came to his notice or whose echoes

[1] *Annals of the Bodleian Library*, p. 6.

chanced to penetrate his seclusion. He tells in quaint ungrammatical Latin how Duke Humphrey with his wife, *Domina Jacoba Ducessa Holandiæ,* attended by a train of three hundred followers, partly English and partly Teutons, came to St. Albans for the Christmas holidays.[1] "Teutons" probably means the Dutch and other Netherlanders who had drifted into Jacqueline's service. The abbot was just then abroad at the Council of Pavia, and the honours of the house were done by the prior, who received the guests with a solemn procession on Christmas Eve. Perhaps his hand was less strong to maintain order in the abbey's jurisdiction for there was much lawlessness, unruliness, and poaching in the neighbourhood during this visit, chiefly on the part of the Duke's retainers. The impetuous Humphrey determined to make an example of one of his servants who was among the culprits. He had the man placed in the stocks,

---

[1] His chronicle is printed with that of Amundesham: *Annales Monasterie S. Albani,* Henry Thomas Riley, editor, Roll series, p. 4; see also *Journ. Brit. Arch.,* 1871. The abbey of St. Albans was at the end of the first day's journey from London on the great north road.

DUKE HUMPHREY'S LIBRARY, OXFORD.

"broke his head with a mattrass beater," and ordered his greyhound to be hanged, as he had been the man's companion in his ne-· farious hunting in the abbey woods. Duke Humphrey was nothing if not strenuous when he felt like it, and the writer may be believed that his summary methods "set at rest this evil appetite for sporting on part of his servants." When they departed, the ducal visitors left two purple robes as a present.[1]

At another time, "on the day of the exaltation of the Holy Cross, after the celebration of vespers, the Duchess of Holland rode through the great court of the abbey attended by twenty-four horsemen, on her way to the royal mansion at Langley, and next day the Duke followed her accompanied by the knight, John Robessart, and ten horsemen."[2]

The years following the marriage were consumed in delays of various kinds on both sides of the Channel, before action was taken

---

[1] See Riley, intr. to Amundesham, p. xvi.
[2] *Ibid.*, p. 8. The dowager queen, Joanna, was living at Langley.

to reinstate the Countess and to determine what ducal title she might rightfully bear. There were many events which militated against Jacqueline's returning with her new husband to demand restitution of her alienated territories.

In Holland the ex-bishop had proved an efficient ruler. He had brought affairs to such comparative quiet that the conditions of trade and manufacture had greatly improved both there and in Zealand. When his hands were freed in those provinces and he could entrust the reins to deputies, he turned his attention to Friesland, of which he styled himself "Lord," as Jacqueline herself "Lady," of the "free Frisians." The question as to the extent of their freedom had been a bone of contention between them and the counts of Holland for many a long year. William VI once gained some advantage only to lose it again, but John actually obtained recognition over one portion of their territory (September 1, 1421) and retained it.

Engrossed as he was in war, this ex-bishop also found time to be a patron of the arts.

It was to painting that he turned his attention, however, rather than to books. In his court the early Dutch artists found asylum and recognition. Jan van Eyck was in his service for about two years. We find his name in the long list of knights, minstrels and servants at The Hague, as my gracious lord's painter—*myn genadichs heeren scilder*.

When the news was brought to John of Bavaria that Jacqueline's conditional promises to Humphrey had been fulfilled without waiting for the satisfaction of the conditions, he was highly shocked. He declared that a grievous insult had been offered to all Christendom. The suit of divorce was pending before the court of Rome. No new marriage was legally possible. This hasty act defied the curia and the civilised world and disgraced the pair

Not long afterwards, John executed an act making Philip of Burgundy his heir and his successor as ruward of Jacqueline's territories. There was apparently no revival of his own ancient claim as count *de facto*. His pretensions rested solely on the mortgage given by John of Brabant, and the investiture of Emperor Sigismund was not mentioned in the deed.

Humphrey paid little attention to his or to other protests. To Philip of Burgundy he applied for aid in restoring his wife to her heritage. All paper and ink sent in that quest were quite wasted, for Burgundy had nothing whatsoever to gain by dispossessing John the uncle. At the same time the situation was complicated, because Philip did not really desire a breach with England, especially as he had recently cemented his friend ship with Humphrey's brother John by giving him the hand of his sister, Anne of Burgundy It is evident, moreover, that Jacqueline's position as doubtful wife of her noble husband could not have been as disgraceful in the eyes of her contemporaries as is represented by Bilderdijk and others. For when this new Duchess of Bedford was naturalised as a native of her husband's country it was also conceded in the name of the little king "to our dearest kinswoman Jacqueline, Duchess of Gloucester, that she

Jacqueline in England

becomes a native *(quod ipsa fiat indigena)* and free to enjoy all rights as though she had been born in England."[1]

Her faithful friend, John Robessart, also became an English subject on the same day (October 20, 1423).[2] At the moment of the issue of these naturalisation briefs Humphrey had succeeded in asserting his claim to more power in the government as guardian of Henry VI than the council desired to concede to him. On October 19th the right to convene Parliament was accorded to him and he thus attained a temporary triumph over his uncle, the Bishop of Winchester, who had opposed him in every step since the death of the late king. Jealousy of Winchester was a large factor in Humphrey's reluctance to relinquish his hold on his nephew's affairs, even temporarily, in order to go abroad to retrieve his wife's fortunes.

Meanwhile John of Brabant—styling himself also Duke of Hainaut—declared his willingness to accept the dukes of Burgundy

---

[1] Rymer's *Fœdera*, x., p. 311. See also Van Mieris, iv., p. 700. Rolls of Parliament, iv., p. 242. [2] Rymer, x., p. 312.

and Bedford as arbitrators in the "difference existing between him and the Duke of Gloucester."¹ If Gloucester should refuse, however, he would not be bound. The Englishman was slow in his deliberations over this proposal. There was something humiliating in its terms. Jacqueline was living as Humphrey's wife and he thought that the legality of their union should be accepted by the family circle without further question.

In September, 1423, Bedford met his new brother-in-law in Paris and promised to use his influence with Humphrey and make him consent to submit to arbitration.

Evidently Bedford succeeded in presenting convincing arguments. On February 15, 1424, Humphrey, "son, brother and uncle of kings², Duke of Gloucester, Count of Haynnau, Hollande, Zeellande, Pembroucq and lord of Friesland, grand chamberlain and also protector and defender of England," in order to "avoid great perils damages and

[1] *Cartulaire,* iv., p. 343. June 16, 1423.
[2] *Ibid.,* p. 368.

irreparable inconveniences," consents to submit the "debate, dissension, and discord between the Duke of Brabant on the one hand and us on the other to our well beloved brother and cousin, the dukes of Bedford and Burgundy." Knowing, however, the law's delays, Humphrey expressly stipulates in this document that the decision must be made by the end of the following March or he would have none of it. The machinery of law moved slowly, however, as was its wont in the fifteenth century. Nothing was decided in March. And May was almost ended when Humphrey agreed to prolong his "obligation contracted Feb. 15" until the end of June.

At that same time[1] Jacqueline gave her pledge to abide by the decisions to be rendered by "our dear brother the regent of France, the Duke of Bedford and our well loved cousin the Duke of Burgundy" on the difference between "our cousin the Duke of Brabant" and "our much revered lord and

---

[1] May 27th. These letters are in the archives at Dijon. *Cartulaire,* iv., pp. 380, 381.

husband the Duke of Gloucester, Count of Hainaut, Holland, Zealand and Pembroucq."[1] Yes, she promised by the "faith and oath of our body and *en parole de princesse*" to accept everything that might be decreed by the brother and cousin. Yet even in her promise she assumed that one man was her husband and bore her titles by virtue of so being, and that the other was merely Duke of Brabant without claim to her estates. Her very words were contradictory.

By the end of June judgment was still hanging fire.[2] Days had been set for hearings several times at Bruges and elsewhere, there were several discussions, but no formal court was held until October, when the arbitrators met at Paris and the case was set forth.[3] Hair-splitting were the arguments. Papal letters were produced stating that Martin V certainly had been misinformed about what would cause trouble and what

[1] *Cartulaire*, iv., p. 380; also p. xxx. The original is at Lille.

[2] It was at Bruges on April 6th that John of Bavaria had declared Philip his heir.—*Cartulaire*, iv., p. 374.

[3] Monstrelet, iv., p. 207. Löher, ii., p. 146. Also *Recueil des croniques d'Angleterre* par Jehan de Waurin (Hardy's edition), v., livre iii., chap. 22. In some cases Waurin seems to copy Monstrelet

would bring peace. Therefore his decrees enacted under misapprehension were invalid, and everything done to the injury of the Brabant marriage was null and void.

Humphrey's advocates steadfastly refused to allow the above assertion to pass. They argued that in revoking his revocation the Pope had far exceeded his powers. It was impossible to confirm a right that had never existed. The latest dispensation, moreover, only referred to two of the hindrances between the parties, but the other points were not mentioned. Jacqueline had never been the legal wife of John of Brabant. With full freedom and honour had she given her hand to Humphrey. *Ergo* the Duke of Brabant was bound to deliver over all her hereditary lands, goods, and revenues to Gloucester as her legal husband. Many more arguments were exchanged. Finally the Brabant duke declared that he would renounce all claim to his former wife if a life interest in Hainaut were conceded to him. After his death the countship might lapse to Humphrey who must assume all Jacqueline's debts, pay the costs of the suit at Rome, and cede Hal, Heusden, and Geertruidenberg to Brabant. No decisive verdict was pronounced. All that the arbitrators decided was that the whole suit, with the new issues made clear at the trial, must be again submitted to the Pope.

Humphrey had gained one point. The legality of his marriage was not expressly denied. That was all, and that was insufficient to satisfy the pair. Nor did Humphrey and Jacqueline intend to be satisfied. They had indeed pledged themselves to accept the decision of the arbitration. But they held that this postponement was no judgment and that there was nothing to abide by. When the opinion was rendered they had already begun to take matters into their own hands and were *en route* for Hainaut. Owing to the French wars and the state of the English exchequer, the Privy Council decided that no troops should be furnished to Humphrey. England's duty was to keep every man and penny for her own immediate needs. But by hook and by crook the Duke

ANNE OF BURGUNDY, DUCHESS OF BEDFORD.

Bedford missal. Photo from original.
British Museum MS. Add., 18850.

Jacqueline in England

succeeded in recruiting a respectable force at his own expense.

In September an embassy sent from Mons[1] to England found the adventurous and errant pair encamped at Dover waiting for a favourable wind.[2] When it blew they sailed pleasantly over to Calais and rumours of their enterprise spread here and there, reaching The Hague on October 21st, where the council were sitting.[3] In Mons the council were also in session and they had more accurate advices than rumour. "This day Saturday [October 21st], after dinner were received two letters which our herald brought us, one from Monsieur of Gloucester and the other from our excellent hereditary Lady, mentioning that they had arrived at Calais in good disposition and that they intended to come to Hainaut to take possession."

[1] De Potter, p. 99.
[2] See *Kröniek* (Hist. Gen. te Utrecht, 1851), p. 260. *Geschiedkundige byzonderheden.*
[3] " Premier régistre des consaux de Mons." *Cartulaire*, iv., p. 413.

CHAPTER VIII

Sovereign in Hainaut

1424

IT was while Humphrey and Jacqueline were at Calais that they learned of the failure of the arbitrators to pronounce a final decision on their suit, and a few messages were exchanged between them and their kinsmen in Paris before they actually set out for Hainaut, in spite of well founded information that the good people of the province did not desire the return of their lady under the existing circumstances.

"On the 24th day of November there departed from Mons, Jehan de le Loge, Jaquemart le Féron, etc., and made their way to Quesnoy to find our said very revered lady the dowager to beg her to intercede with our very respected lady her daughter and request her, please, not to come to the town of Mons nor to bring M. of Gloucester with her without the knowledge and consent of the Estates."[1]

The envoys reached Quesnoy only to learn that the dowager had already departed for Bouchain, and that by that time she had joined her daughter and the Duke of Gloucester, and all three were travelling towards Mons. The worthy citizens hastened to follow the same route and they succeeded in coming up with the party at Crespin, where their city's message was duly delivered. But "notwithstanding the remonstrances" the "hereditary lady" continued her journey. It was on Monday, November 27th, that they left Crespin and they were received in Mons on the same day. The ducal pair with an escort were installed in the Naasterhof, but they consented, at the request of the city, to leave the major part of their forces to lodge in the faubourgs of Mons. "On Wednesday after dinner our hereditary lady and the Duke of Gloucester

[1] *Cartulaire,* iv., p. 419.

went to see the garden of the archery gild and gave a present of six nobles to aid in enlarging the chapel," and then Jacqueline took the Duke upon the hill in the park to have a view and afterwards they visited the castle.[1] She was at home again, and proud to show her English husband her capital.

Thus the city received the sovereign and her new duke in spite of previous protests, and the authorities expended ninety-four pounds and three shillings in wine to drink their health. The city fathers evidently determined to make the best of an unwelcome situation.

There was little delay in convening the Estates of Hainaut. On December 1st, they were in session in the Naasterhof. Then, in the name of Jacqueline, the sub-prior, Jan l'Orfevre, delivered an harangue setting forth the reason why her alleged marriage to John of Brabant was null and void.[2] It was true, indeed, that Rome had lately given dispensation anew in regard to two of the four points

---
[1] *Cartulaire*, iv., p. 420.
[2] *Résolutions du conseil de ville.* De Potter, note, 102, and *Cartulaire*, iv., p. 422.

already urged and dispensation might be obtained for the other two, but still the marriage had never been valid in the past and Jacqueline, of course, no longer desired to make it so. In consenting to the Brabant union, the princess felt she had stained her conscience. She had now cleansed herself from her sin in confession and had received forgiveness under condition of giving twelve hundred French crowns to charity and of performing penance. These conditions she had duly fulfilled. Later, in accordance with the advice of learned theologians and lay scholars, she had entered into a union with the Duke of Gloucester which had now existed about two years and given rise to no opposition (?). On this ground she demanded that her true and legitimate husband, Humphrey of Gloucester, should be received as regent and governor in Hainaut (*mambour et avoué*).

The opinion of the assembly was that the session was hardly sufficiently full to take the responsibility of so weighty a decision. A little delay ensued while missing members were summoned to fill their seats. The discussion was renewed and on December 4th, after a heated debate, the princess's statement was accepted. No time was allowed to lag. On the very next day, December 5th, the Duke of Gloucester was formally recognised as Count of Hainaut, and at the same time he received homage as regent in behalf of his wife.[1]

Then the Estates wrote to the Duke of Brabant that there was reciprocal release from all oaths given and taken between him and the people of Hainaut.

This decision was accepted by the majority of the cities of Hainaut. Soignies, Mauberge, Quesnoy, Valenciennes, were ready to offer their homage to Humphrey and Jacqueline The city of Hal, two members of the families of Edingen, and the Lord of Jeumont adhered to John of Brabant, but the Lord of Havré, John's own commander-in-chief in Hainaut, joined Jacqueline's standard.

Thus was the titular Count of Hainaut dispossessed. Dynter represents him as wait

[1] *Cartulaire*, iv., p. 425.

ing like a pious Christian gentleman for the final decree of the Church to which he was obedient, highly indignant at Humphrey's refusal to abide by the Paris arbitration.[1] The Brabanter, on receiving official news of the new footing on which he had been placed in Hainaut, straightway sent off plaintive messages to his uncle in Holland and to his cousin of Burgundy. The latter needed no spur to enter the field against Humphrey. When news was brought to him from Calais that the latter had thrown all considerations of policy to the winds and was actually on the road to claim Hainaut, accompanied by his wife and by an army to make good his claim, Philip was furious, and declared that henceforth he would aid John of Brabant to the full extent of his power. Humphrey had broken his word and need expect no further consideration from any Christian. Humphrey, on his part, was still disposed to avoid offending his cousin Philip more than he could help. "In passing through the country of the Duke of Burgundy he restrained

[1] Dynter, vi., cap. 207.

his men from injury and would suffer them to do naught but to lodge and take victuals and drink courteously."[1]

While these events were passing, one foe of Jacqueline's was removed from her path. In the summer of 1424, before the errant countess had turned her face homeward, a plot had been hatched against the life of her uncle John, the ex-bishop. Jan van Vliet, the second husband of Jacqueline's half-sister Beatrice, was involved in this and convicted of the crime. We have the story as he is said to have told it in his confession.[2]

"On Ascension day Jan van Vliet was at Schoonhoven, and on Friday he supped with John the Bastard of Langeraek." After supper a group of men strolled along the river and Van Vliet fell into conversation with an English merchant who was of the party. "Can you speak French?" said the latter. "No." "Latin, then?" "No." "Then you are only half a man," rejoined the merchant. Some medium of communication

---

[1] Monstrelet, iv., p. 210. Waurin, vol. v., liv., iii., ch. 32.
[2] Van Mieris, iv., p. 729. Dynter, vi., cap. 208.

was found, however, and the Englishman contrived to make it clear to the Hollander that he understood the fact of his enmity to John of Bavaria, and that he was ready to make it worth his while to rid the land of the obnoxious ex-prelate, besides furnishing him the means. Van Vliet met these advances willingly. Poison was provided from England and given to him wrapped in a doeskin bag enclosed in a little casket. Van Vliet found an opportunity of possessing himself of the ruward's prayer-book and, protecting his hand with a glove, he smeared the poison on the pages. He then threw the box into a vault and burned the glove, besides rubbing his hands on a wall and taking care not to touch food with his fingers for some time. The poison was only strong enough to make Duke John ill without killing him. Owing to this failure, Van Vliet was refused the two thousand crowns promised him. How the story leaked out does not appear, but by July, Van Vliet was arrested and examined in prison at Purmerende by the Duke's privy councillor and deputies from the four chief cities. Later he was taken to The Hague, where he repeated his confession before the Court of Holland where sat Frank and Floris van Borselen, Philip of Cortgene, and other barons, including a few from Luxemburg. In addition deputies from ten of the chief Holland towns were present. The circumstances were plain and John van Woerden, Lord Van Vliet, was condemned to death and suffered his sentence on August 3, 1424. All details of the punishment ordinarily imposed for treason against a sovereign were enforced.[1]

Duke John dragged on a miserable existence for some months, feeling his strength broken and his end near In September he tried to provide for his future reputation and spiritual welfare by confirming anew all privileges and charters granted by him or by his predecessors to the dean and chapter of the chapel in the palace at The Hague, "to the end that they should remember the souls of his parents[2] and himself in the service

---

[1] The statement in Van Mieris was not drawn up until after John of Bavaria's death. [2] Van Mieris, iv., p. 733.

Sovereign in Hainaut 121

of God" At the entreaty of the Duke of Brabant, he also took heed to things of this world and began to make preparations to aid his nephew in repelling the imminent invasion of his territories. Epiphany was appointed as the date for the muster of his troops, the very time, however, when the ruward was forced to meet the summons of Fate in his own person. On January 6, 1425, suddenly he fell dead. He was in the midst of this world's business. Only the day before he had been arranging about the payment for certain jewels, his New Year's gifts to his wife and her ladies, while at the moment when he breathed his last he was on his way to his newly levied army. The death was unhesitatingly attributed to the slow effects of the poison administered in July. The four quarters of Van Vliet's body hung rotting on the gates of the chief cities of Holland in ghastly reminder of the murderous purpose of the executed man even while the victim had apparently escaped[1]

---

[1] Goudhoeven, *Chron. van Holland.* Van Mieris, iv., p. 730. The leg sent to Leyden remained on the gate for a year and then was burned.

the danger. After he succumbed to it, the rumours regarding the real agent of the plot against his life were revived. Van Vliet had had plenty of reason for disliking the ruward on his own behalf, but no one charged him with being the principal in the crime. There were suspicions that the deed was plotted in England, that the poisoner was urged on by his sister's wrongs and not by his own grievances, and that Jacqueline herself was not innocent of actual complicity in her uncle's death. But there was no proof of her guilt, though she could not have regretted the decease of one who had wronged her with all the means in his power.

Her actual gain, however, proved nothing. John of Brabant hastened to The Hague to take possession of the lands lapsed to him by the ruward's death as well as of those willed to him directly. On February 8, 1425, he proceeded to confirm all previous charters and privileges and heaped favours on the nobles, identifying himself entirely with the Cod party.[1] The animus of his every

---
[1] Dynter, vi., cap. 209. Van Mieris, iv., p. 747, etc.

CARDINAL BEAUFORT, BISHOP OF WINCHESTER.
From a painting by J. Parker in the collection of Horace Walpole.

action came, however, from Philip of Burgundy, whose way to his desired goal began to seem clear. Jacqueline was passed over in silence in her uncle's will, and Philip was named as heir after John of Brabant, who was already so very feeble that he could hardly sit a horse. He counted for little. Had it not been for Burgundy, Holland and Zealand would have undoubtedly returned to the obedience of Jacqueline. There were confident expectations that the Pope was about to declare Humphrey the legal husband of his unfortunate wife, and then the land could hope to have a strong-handed governor and protector. The cities were divided as to their action. Some acknowledged John of Brabant at once, others held back. Dordrecht and Zierikzee, for example, declared themselves neutral. It was Schoonhoven that became the headquarters of Jacqueline's party, and thither flocked the discontented in numbers, but there was little formal response to the open letters issued jointly by Humphrey and Jacqueline calling on cities and nobles to aid their cause.

CHAPTER IX

Hopes and Fears

1425

WITH the disappearance of the ex-bishop from the scene, Philip of Burgundy felt a greater personal interest at stake in the general conflict of interests, and he neglected no means in his power calculated to annoy or embarrass the man whose rivalry he feared. This was at the epoch when it was considered a virtuous action to enlist in the war against the heretical Hussites. From the pulpit, priests were in the habit of urging the faithful to volunteer or to contribute funds to aid in campaigns against pernicious heretics, just as they had preached crusades against the Turks. At the instigation of Philip, similar means were employed to urge Hainauters to assume arms against the Englishman who defied the Church by taking to himself the wife of another. These sermons, which put him on a par with Turks and heretics and ranked his opponents as pious crusaders fighting a righteous battle, roused Humphrey's bitter anger. The rumours of such personal attacks were perhaps indefinite for a time, but when there fell into his hands one of the broadsides issued by Duke Philip, summoning all able to bear arms to join the standard of John of Luxemburg, who was about to repel Humphrey's iniquitous invasion, the latter seized his pen and proceeded to protest vigorously against his cousin's action. The text of the wordy epistles that passed between the two princes is given in Monstrelet, taken from copies seen by that author.[1] The whole correspondence is an odd chapter in Jacqueline's story.

Humphrey's first letter is written in "My city of Mons, under my seal January 12th." The tenor of the contents is that he can hardly believe that the proclamation which he encloses actually emanated from Duke

[1] iv., p. 213, etc.

Philip even though it is dated from Dijon, because, forsooth, it is full of lies, and his said cousin would not deviate so far from the truth. Who was better aware than Philip how ready Gloucester had been to accept the decision of the arbitrators upon the differences between him and the Duke of Brabant? "*You* know what offers I have made even to my disadvantage, to which, as you know, the party of the Duke of Brabant would not listen nor would they make any accommodation. . . . And you know, too, if consanguinity is to influence you in your action, that you ought to be inclined to help my cause, considering that my companion and wife is doubly your first cousin and my cousin of Brabant is not so near of kin to you. Moreover, you are bound to me by a treaty of peace which you and I solemnly swore to preserve. On the other hand no such compact exists between you and the Duke of Brabant. Nay more, he has entered into alliances which would naturally excite you against him. I have not broken our compact and never shall

. . . If I have injured my cousin of Brabant it is not my fault, as you know, but his attacks have forced me to do what lies in my power to defend my honour and my country. As to the truth, you know already what is patent to all the world, etc.

Therefore high and powerful prince, most worthy and much loved cousin, let me know your intentions by the bearer of this and also whether I can do anything for your service. I will busy myself therein with all my heart. Our Lord, whose protection for you I pray, knows it."

Philip had nothing ready for the return messenger, in accordance with Humphrey's request. His answer was delayed until March 3d, but it is unequivocal. He acknowledges the letters patent and proclamations as issued by him, declares roundly that it was the Duke of Brabant who had accepted, and Gloucester who had refused, the decree of the Paris tribunal, that it was John who was right and Humphrey who was wrong, because, without awaiting the Pope's final decision on the legality of his marriage he had "fallen on Hainaut with an armed force and tried to drive out my Brabant cousin and to rob him of his lawful possessions." Philip demands that Humphrey shall retract all expressions insulting to his truth and to his honour, and then suggests that, in case Humphrey persists in his damaging assertions, it might be better for them, "two young knights as we are," to put an end to the quarrel in single combat and to avoid spilling Christian blood. Ignoring the fact that he had delayed weeks before replying to Humphrey's urgent letter, in his turn, the Duke of Burgundy is impatient and demands an immediate answer by bearer. He did not have it. Nearly a fortnight elapses before Humphrey's response from Soignies. The contents were as follows:

"*High and Mighty Prince Philip, Duke of Burgundy, Count of Flanders, Count of Artois and Burgundy.*

"I, Humphrey, Son, Brother, and Uncle to the Kings of England, Duke of Gloucester

Count of Hainaut, Holland and Zealand, and Pembroke, Lord of Friesland, and Grand Chamberlain of the King of England, have received your letters in the form of a placard addressed to me, written on the third instant, duly signed with your name and sealed to assure me that its contents come from your knowledge and at your instance.

"Recapitulation of its contents seems to me as little worth while as to you seemed repetition of my letter written from my good city of Mons in my countship of Hainaut under my seal on January 12th. But when your letter asserts that I have, as you say, refused to lay aside my quarrel with my cousin the Duke of Brabant, I must declare that is less than the truth. For my dear brother, the regent, and the entire French council are perfectly aware of what my action has been and you know it too, and you cannot deny it if you want to. And as to your charges that I accuse you falsely and mendaciously . . . I assure you that I will stand by my letter and maintain it as true. Moreover . . . it is confirmed by what your people have done and perpetrated in my countship. Not for you, not for any man will I go back on my word. Therefore will I, with the help of God, of the Virgin, and of my patron St. George acknowledge and stand by the contents of my letter—will stake my body against yours on its truth, before either of the arbitrators whom you have chosen—Both are the same to me.

"And as to your demand that we should make short work of our affair—that, too, is exactly what I wish, and as my dear brother[1] is near at hand I am quite content to submit the matter to him and accept him as an arbitrator. . . . If, however, my brother will not take part in the affair, then I am content that it shall go before the very high and mighty prince, the Emperor, and if he refuse, before my brother-in-law Adalbert or some other impartial judge. Because I do not know whether you will hold by your signet, so I ask and demand that you send me another letter by the bearer of this, sealed

---

[1] This is *beaufrère* in Monstrelet, iv., p. 221, but evidently it is Bedford who is meant.

with your state seal as this letter is sealed with mine.

"And as for the Brabanter, if you continue to assert that he has more right in this contest than I, then am I ready to declare—my body against yours—on the day [St. George's] and before the judges aforesaid, that I have and will have better right by the Grace of God, of Our Lady, and of St. George.

"And as a token that I count and maintain all this as upright have I set my name thereto and my state seal. Written in my city of Soignies, March 16, 1425"

This time Philip's response is immediate and written on the same day, March 16th. He throws Humphrey's words back in his teeth, reasserts his own position in an arrogant fashion, and expatiates on his hearty sympathy for his injured cousin of Brabant. He accepts Humphrey's challenge in a deprecating manner as though he himself had not suggested the duel, and agrees to St. George's Day (April 23d) as the date, subject to the approval of the Duke of Bedford.

Letters on the subject were not confined to the chief parties. The University of Paris wrote to the Duke of Burgundy, to the Privy Council, and to English prelates, urging that the quarrel be not allowed to come to the point of a duel. The arguments are most copious and classic quotations abound.[1]

Meantime other events had taken place. On February 3d, the Estates of Hainaut convened at the call of the English duke, who delivered an harangue on the need of absolute union between Holland, Zealand, and Hainaut, and exhorted the loyal subjects of himself and his wife to write at once to her northern provinces and bring them to their duty. After this, taxes were imposed and a few were collected, but a state of war, or uncertainty worse than war, prevailed throughout Hainaut. The English soldiers overran the territory and the inhabitants did not know which evil to choose. Little by little, however, Jacqueline's cause lost ground. Sometimes, as it seemed, by

[1] *Journal des Savants,*—1899, p. 191 *et seq.*

sheer ill luck. Braine-le-Comte, a town that held stoutly to her cause, was besieged by the Count of St. Pol in behalf of his brother, the Duke of Brabant. The English garrison placed there by Humphrey was strong in its position, when suddenly on the eighth day of the siege they yielded up the city, which paid a heavy penalty for its resistance. Later, some of the prisoners were questioned as to the reason for their capitulation, unexpected and unnecessary, especially as in earlier attacks they had displayed such sturdiness. Their answer was that they had not had the remotest intention of surrendering, when, to their terror and amazement, they saw St. George himself riding among the invaders. Then they knew that God was against them and that there was no further use in holding out. It was no vision, only a case of mistaken identity. Among the Brabanters was one Daniel de Bouchout, whose own arms were almost the same as those of St. George. The fact that he rode a beautiful white horse completed the illusion and superstition conquered where strength would have failed.[1] John of Brabant recognised the aid rendered by the good citizens of Bois-le-Duc in this siege by the present of a twelve branched candelabra.

There was a growing public sentiment against the righteousness of Jacqueline's cause. A league actually sprang into being among her opponents. A tiny silver shield attached to the right arm distinguished the young nobles of this brotherhood. The sun emblazoned on the shield signified that the Duke of Brabant's rights were as clear as the sun. Now John of Brabant was no heroic figure and it is hard to believe that adherents adopted his cause for personal love of him. This warm partisanship was fictitious, and behind the fiction undoubtedly stood the ingenious and ever ready Philip of Burgundy. Strange how little compassion was apparently excited by the dispossessed Countess whose fate was so full of pathos.

---

[1] Dynter, vi., cap. 211. *Brabantsche Yeesten,* vii., verse 15197 *et seq.* See too, *Mémoires de Pierre de Fenin,* p. 231. (Fenin b. 1385, d. 1433. Prévôt of Arras.)

TWELVE-BRANCHED CANDELABRA PRESENTED TO THE CITIZENS OF
BOIS LE DUC.   1424 O. S.

Dame Jacque la désirée she was called in the camps, but there is a tone of derision in the term.[1]

While Philip and Humphrey were exhausting their stock of epistolary epithets upon each other, new letters came from Rome dated February 13, 1425. Martin V hastened to disavow all the proclamations purporting to come from him which had been published in Jacqueline's territory and which asserted the legality of her English marriage. All were forgeries and the divorce was still pending. He orders Jacqueline to leave Humphrey and remain under the charge of some neutral prince.[2] There is no doubt as to the reason for this mandatory brief. Philip of Burgundy had plenty of very convenient gossips in his service who could carry news or rumours wheresoever and whensoever he wished. At this crisis any barrier to Jacqueline's acquisition of

---

[1] The authorities for statements like this are mainly Burgundian. In Valenciennes, however, among her own people there was sharp opposition. There a broadside was circulated showing Dame Reason telling Humphrey that he was more criminal than his father, the regicide, or his brother who tried to steal France. (See Löher ii., p. 192.)

[2] Dynter, vi., cap. 214.

friends or of reputation in the Netherlands was important to him and the Pope's letter, undoubtedly written at his direct instigation, was a timely damper to hopes cherished by Jacqueline that her equivocal status was to be speedily settled at Rome in accordance with her fervent wishes.

The loss of Braine-le-Comte was serious; then followed a truce to last until the much talked of duel of St. George's Day. Meanwhile urgent letters came from England beseeching Humphrey to return. He was torn in two directions, but the reasons for going proved the more cogent. He had no desire to abandon his hold on his royal nephew's affairs by too long an absence from London, he wanted new accoutrements so as to make a brave appearance when he met Burgundy in the duel, he was restrained from pressing on to Holland and Zealand as he desired, he was losing faith in the chances, that the legality of his marriage would soon be duly established, he was tired of his own position, uncertain in spite of the display of his titles, and perhaps, too, he was a little weary of his impetuous wife, who was probably not a very soothing companion in these days when the tide of her affairs seemed to have turned for the worse

Whatever his exact motive or mixture of motives, however, Duke Humphrey set off for England about April 12th.[1] There was rejoicing in Hainaut when he took away his troops, who had preyed sadly on the land, but the titular mistress of the province did not share in the joy. She and her mother with an escort of sixteen horse accompanied Humphrey as far as Crespin, for Jacqueline could not bear to say farewell to her husband at St. Ghislain, as first proposed. To Mons Jacqueline then sadly returned alone, and on Monday, April 30th, according to the records,[2] she appeared before the municipal council and made an appeal in person for their aid. Certainly her stress was dire.

[1] Waurin is an authority for the statement that with him went Eleanor Cobham, one of Jacqueline's English ladies-in-waiting, who would not stay longer in foreign parts (v., chap. 37).

Particularités Curieuses sur Jacqueline de Bavière, i., p. 112; Fenin, p. 234; Monstrelet, iv., part ii., chap. 29; St. Remy, ii., chap. 145; *Beitrage*, pp. 64, 65; Stow, *Chron.*, p. 367; *Cartulaire*, iv., p. xxxvi., etc.   [2] *Cartulaire*, iv , p. 462.

The nets stretched by Burgundy and Brabant were being drawn tighter about her. Her cause was a lost one when she wrote the following letter to her English husband. Her choice of terms in addressing him are filial rather than wifely.[1]

"My much feared seigneur and father, as humbly as I can and know how to do I recommend myself to your kindness. And pray know, my most excellent lord and father, that I write now to your lordship as the most unhappy, the most ruined and falsely treated woman alive. For, my most respected seigneur, on Sunday, June 13,[2] the deputies of your city of Mons returned and brought a treaty drafted and signed between our fine cousins of Burgundy and Brabant, which treaty was made in the absence of my mother and without her knowledge, as she has herself assured me through Master Gérard le Grand, her chaplain. Therefore,

---

[1] All authors take this letter to Humphrey from Monstrelet, iv., p. 235.
[2] XIII. Thus it stands in Monstrelet and is repeated in Van Mieris, iv., p. 783. Löher corrects to *third*. See also *Cartulaire—troisième;* iv., p. 475. As April 29th fell on Sunday so did June 3d; June 13th is Wednesday.

respected seigneur, my mother has written letters regarding the same treaty about which she did not venture to advise me, for she herself did not know what to do, but she begged me to ask my good people of this city to find out what consolation and aid they could furnish me.

"Thereupon, much loved lord and father, I went on the following morning to the council chamber and reminded them how you, at their own desire and prayer, had consented to leave me under their care and protection as people who had sworn that they would be your true and faithful subjects, trusting them to shelter me and to give you reckoning thereof, according to the oath they had sworn by the sacrament of the altar and on the holy gospels. Thereupon, my honoured lord and father, they answered roundly that they were not strong enough to protect me. And at the same time, confirming their words with deeds, they arose and said that my people wanted to murder them. And it went so far, my dread lord, that they seized one of your subjects, Sergeant Macart, and had him beheaded in my very presence. Then they arrested all who love you and belong to your party, such as Bardoul de la Porte, his brother Colard, Gillet de la Porte, Jean du Bois, Guillaume de Leeur, Sanson, your sergeant, Pierre Baron, Sandrart, Dandre, and others of your followers to the number of two hundred and fifty.

"They also intend to arrest Heer Baudouin, the treasurer, Heer Louis de Montfort, Haulvère, Jehan Fresne, and Estienne d'Istre. They have not yet done this but I do not know what they may still do. Also they said without circumlocution, that if I would not come to an agreement they would deliver me into the hands of my fine cousin of Brabant. I only have permission to stay in this city eight days, before I am forced to go to Flanders, which is very grievous and hard for me, for I greatly doubt whether I shall ever see you again in my whole life unless you come to my aid in all haste.

"Ah, my dread lord and father, all my hopes and expectations are in your control;

Hopes and Fears 141

you are my only and sovereign joy and all that I suffer is from love of you. So I implore you humbly and as tenderly as one can in this world, that for God's sake you may have pity on me and my misery and come to aid me, your forlorn creature, as speedily as possible, if you do not wish to lose me for ever. I hope that you will do this. For, my dread lord and father, I have not deserved otherwise of you and as long as I live I shall never do anything that could displease you. Yes, I am ready at any moment to encounter death from love of you and your noble person, for your lordship is all my delight. By my faith, my dread lord and prince, my sole consolation, and my last hope, may it please you for the love of God and of our patron Saint George, to consider as speedily as you can my dolorous affairs. This you have not yet done, for, as it seems, you have wholly forgotten me.

"For the moment I know nothing else to write, except that I have sent Lord Louis de Montfort in all haste to you, for, although he remains true to me when all others forsake me, he cannot stay here longer. He will tell you all in more detail than I can write. Therefore I implore you, very worthy lord and father, be a good master to him, and let me know your wish, which I will obey with my whole soul.

"My witness is the blessed son of God, who may give you a long and happy life, and grant me the favour of seeing you again to my great joy.

"Written in the false and treacherous city of Mons with a deeply sorrowful heart on the sixth day of June.

"Your sorrowing and beloved child, who suffers unspeakably for your sake. Your daughter of
"QUENNBOURG." [1]

To her cousin Louis, Count Palatine, then in London, Jacqueline also wrote a short letter [2]:

[1] Löher considers that *Quennbourg* is simply a mistake of the copyist for *Pembroucq*, one of Humphrey's titles. (*Beiträge*, p. 83.) In some editions it is "Quienbourg." Gachard, in *Barante, Hist. des Ducs de Bourgogne*, i., 456, note 2, doubts whether the letter as given by Monstrelet is genuine, owing to the date, June 13th. That is, however, evidently a mere slip, as other circumstances fix the dates.

[2] Monstrelet, iv., p. 238. See also Vinchant, *Annales de la province et comté du Haynaut*, vi., p. 164. The signature occurs in the two forms.

"Very worthy beloved cousin. I commend myself to your protection. Know that at the writing of this letter I am in great trouble as a woman falsely and treacherously betrayed. And as you desire to have tidings, my very worthy and beloved cousin, know that at present I can do no more than repeat what I have already written. Please ask our very dear and dread lord, who can tell you more than you may like to hear. Otherwise I could not help repeating, except to beg you keep your hand to that which you know, so that my dread lord may come, otherwise neither you nor he will ever see me again.

"And as to your advice to me to cross the sea, it is too late; do you hasten hither with a good force that you may free me out of the hands of the Flemish, where I will be in eight days. Beloved and dear cousin, I pray God that he may give you a fair life and a long one. Written in the false and treacherous city of Mons, June 6th.

"Your cousin,
"JACQUELINE OF QUENNEBROUCH."

In London, meanwhile, Humphrey was received with bitter reproaches that he had allowed his private concerns to jeopardise the holiest interests of his nephew, of his brother, of England. Never again should he have troops to fight against Philip. Humphrey found himself assailed by criticism on all sides, and, unless he were willing to allow his uncle of Winchester once for all to arrogate all his powers to himself, it was evident that he must stay on English soil to hold his ground. He was obliged to postpone the date of the duel, a postponement that suited Philip perfectly.

The reports heard by Jacqueline were true. Mons had been forced to sacrifice her interests to its own safety, and to yield after a brief siege. A treaty arranged at Douay between *beau cousin de Bourgogne* and *beau cousin de Brabant* was indeed most injurious to Jacqueline, since her quondam husband was restored to her sovereignty of Hainaut and she was entrusted to the "protection" of Philip. She humbled herself so far as to appeal to that ex-husband through th

Count of Nassau. She begged him to take her to Brabant rather than to deliver her over to the guardianship of her too-powerful cousin. She might have spared her breath and her humiliation. To Flanders she was forced to go, and thither she journeyed under the escort of the Prince of Orange at the head of five hundred troops.

It was on Wednesday, June 13th, at two o'clock that the countess left the Naasterhof and rode sadly away from her "false and treacherous capital." An item in the books of Mons shows that twenty-eight wagons were provided to carry her furniture, jewels, and baggage.[1] As she passed the windmill near Ath, on the road to Ghent, there was an attempt to rescue her, but the Prince of Orange was on his guard, and her friends were easily overpowered. After she was fairly out of the way, the Duke of Brabant appeared in the neighbourhood of Mons. A little delay to make a few stipulations "for self-protection," and then there were gay festivals

---

[1] *Meubles et jeulviaux et baghages* (*Cartulaire*, iv., p. 481), etc.

when the worthy citizens entered into the obedience of the former husband of their sometime sovereign lady, and within a few weeks her name disappears as a factor in civic affairs from the municipal records of the capital of Hainaut.[1] Duke John appointed the Burgundian commander, John of Luxemburg, as stadtholder of Hainaut—an appointment that revealed the guiding spring of his action if further indications were needed.

[1] See Philip's letters, *Cartulaire,* etc., iv., p. 477.

CHAPTER X

In Prison and Out

WHEN the cavalcade forming Jacqueline's escort reached Ghent, the unhappy lady was lodged in the Grafenstein, an old fortress built at the time of Emperor Otto the Great, and used for many years as residence by the counts of Flanders. By the fifteenth century it was abandoned for a more modern palace. Its ancient black walls rose from the middle of the town. Below, it was furnished with underground passages leading from the cellar to the city walls through which troops could be brought at need. Since the building had ceased to be a dwelling, it had been employed as a prison, though it is said that the rooms were also put to pleasanter usage, as studios for the two Van Eycks when they were at work on the *Adoration of the Lamb.* At the best it was a dreary place and its choice as Jacqueline's residence did not augur well for the kind of care to be given by her self-constituted protector. Thinking that she was no longer an active factor in affairs, with Humphrey safe across the channel, the Duke of Burgundy thought he saw his way clear to obtaining the greater authority in the Netherlands which he had long desired.

At this moment a certain similarity in dynastic conditions prevailed in four groups of Netherland territories. Count Dietrich in Namur, Elizabeth of Gorlitz in Luxemburg, Jacqueline in Holland, Zealand, and Hainaut, John in Brabant with the affiliated states, were all alike in being childless. To all these rulers, Philip of Burgundy was either next of kin or declared heir. It was, therefore, not unnatural that there was a disposition among the people to look ahead to the time when all these uncertainties should be certain and Philip, unequivocally, the chief of all. It was not surprising that the harassed citizens showed some inclination to antici-

THE GRAFENSTE N.

pate the day when his great armies should be a protection instead of a menace to the exposed frontier towns.

While, on one hand, there were reports that no more English troops and money were to be provided in Humphrey's cause, there were also counter rumours. In July a fine tale was told the stadtholder of Hainaut by an English exile — a tale bristling with details that apparently vouched for its truth.[1] For a hundred years nothing had caused so much excitement in England as the fashion in which Humphrey had been treated in Hainaut, in the territory of his lawful wife. Eighty thousand gold pieces besides twenty thousand bowmen had been offered to aid Gloucester in a new campaign. The Scotch king had lately wed Humphrey's cousin and had pledged himself in his marriage contract to furnish his kinsman with eight thousand men. From Ireland too, the same number were coming and every English soldier now on French soil had promised to hasten to the Netherlands at the first

[1] Dynter, vi., cap. 220, etc.

news of Humphrey's landing · All this and more was said by the exile fresh from London. His words were carried to various quarters. Some who heard, nodded wisely and said that English merchants from Calais had talked much in the same strain. Fear lest this might be true caused a half belief in its verity and strengthened apprehensions that already existed. Possibly the reports were made in Burgundy with the direct purpose of paving the way for acceptance of a definite compact sealed by Jacqueline's foes to her prejudice. On July 19th, John of Brabant signed a deed appointing the Duke of Burgundy as Ruward of Holland and Zealand.[1]

On July 25, 1425, a birthday spent by Jacqueline in the sombre fortress of Ghent, her former husband issued letters patent to the Hollanders and Zealanders requesting them to obey the Duke of Burgundy, to whom he had committed the govern-

---

[1] The chancellor of Brabant refused to allow the official seal to be appended to this document. A new one was made for the purpose. *Beiträge*, p. 84; Dynter, vi., cap. 122.

ment of his lands for a term of years. No time was lost by the new Ruward and Heir of Holland, Zealand, and Friesland, as the omnivorous Burgundian hastened to style himself in addition to his former titles. He gathered a fleet at Sluis, besides a picked force of two thousand, and set out for the new countries of "his obedience." Like an army of carrier pigeons, his letters preceded him bearing his thanks to those who had invited him "to liberate the land" There was no dearth of assurances that Philip would confirm existing privileges. Moreover he offered to assume all debts left by the late John of Bavaria.[1] When it suited his purpose he was right royal with gracious promises and Burgundian gold.[2] The Cod party was quite ready to accept him, and they were the strongest now as their numbers had increased under John of Bavaria.

How much the prisoner heard of what was passing does not appear. She certainly

[1] *Kroniek*, "Hist. Genoot te Utrecht," 1851, p. 272.
[2] This appears in the *Recette générale de Hainaut*. *Ibid.*

was not cut off from all outside communication, as is evident from her letters to her English husband on June 19th, telling him of her stress. But she had no part in the world about her. Her English brother-in-law, John, Duke of Bedford, with his Burgundian wife, visited Flanders that summer and they were right sumptuously entertained by Philip and by his new lady, Bonne of Artois. The Duchess of Bedford had been naturalised in England on the same day as the Duchess of Gloucester, but fortune looked on them with a different face, and the luckless sister-in-law certainly did not mingle in the gay doings which celebrated the visit of Anne to her brother. Apparently, however, through the prison walls, there penetrated whispers of Philip's further intentions in Jacqueline's regard, intentions not thwarted by her brother of Bedford. There was talk of sending her to Lille, later to Savoy, where she would be under neutral protection. Ghent was in dangerous proximity to Holland and to England. Even if Philip received general homage he was perfectly conscious that there would always be a chance of fresh Hook plots against him, and the risk would be doubled if the presence of the hereditary princess offered a tempting rallying-point for the disaffected.

This plan of removing her into a more permanent place of detention roused Jacqueline's apprehension and she found means to take matters into her own hand to remove herself out of her cousin's reach. In some way she established communication with her Hook friends in Holland. The importance of her immediate escape was evident and two gentlemen, Arnold Spierinck of Aalborcht and Vos from Delft, so runs one story,[1] offered to rescue their lady. Disguised as merchants they journeyed to Ghent, taking extra horses laden with wares. Having engaged lodging in the city, they loitered around the Grafenstein until they attracted Jacqueline's notice

---

[1] *Codex Tegernseer,* p. 21. Other names are given by some authors, Waurin says that Jacqueline was *comme prisonière eslargie en la ville de Gand,* when she made her escape. It is of course possible that she was not held in actual captivity.

Through her window she recognised them as old friends, and in some fashion managed to receive the bundle of clothes that they carried concealed beneath their cloaks. On an appointed night the princess ordered her bath-room heated that she might take a bath. This was duly reported, and while her guards believed that their charge was safe in the room whose lights they could see from their post, she escaped through an unguarded door, attended by a maid clad like herself in the page's dress provided by the pretended merchants. Unnoticed in this disguise, the two women walked through the streets and out of the city gates.

The Hollanders awaited them with four horses freed from the traders' packs. All mounted and rode away at full speed through the night. None took rest till dawn when they found themselves at the banks of the Scheldt with Antwerp's towers in sight. A boat lay hidden in the rushes, left for them as prearranged. With this they crossed the river and entered the city. At an appointed place they found a wagon

THE FLIGHT OF THE DUCHESS.
August 31, 1525.

and within it a couple of gowns such as were worn by women of the middle class. The two pages transformed themselves into burgher dames, and, seated in the rough conveyance, continued their journey to Breda, where they took a brief rest and then hastened on, weary though they were, to Vianen which they reached before sunrise on the fourth day. Here they were safe on the territory of Henry, Lord of Vianen, a staunch supporter of the Hook cause. He hastened to kiss Jacqueline's hand and to offer his services, while his wife brought out the best garments that her wardrobe contained and aided the fugitive princess to attire herself as better befitted her rank.

"And when the departure of the lady came to the knowledge of Duke Philip he was deeply troubled," says Monstrelet.[1] Well he might be. It is always troublesome to have one's pet plans upset by the unfeeling egoism of other people. Philip found it very annoying to have his cousin

---

[1] *La Chronique,* iv., ii., ch. 35. Dynter and his rhyming echo make little of the event.

rush into the midst of things in her headlong and inconvenient fashion.

The news was also promptly carried to Humphrey.

"On Sunday, September 2d, there departed from the said town of Ghent Pierre the clerk of the receiver and went to England to my said lord [Gloucester] to tell him of the departure of my lady from the city of Ghent, which was a Friday in the night the last day of August, and he came from my said lord by his command and returned to Holland and found my lady in the city of Gouda to whom he delivered the letters of my said lord."[1]

Prisoner though she was, and deprived even of her jewels, Jacqueline contrived to borrow money before she left Ghent, as appears by a receipt dated two years later (February 22, 1427), acknowledging forty-four pounds received by Victor de la Faucille in return for the sum "which I lent to my said lady when she departed lately from the

[1] *Comptes de la recette générale de Hainaut.* "Hist. Gen. te Utrecht," 1851, p. 273.

city of Ghent."[1] With the best aid that a few faithful friends could give, it was still a frightfully unequal contest into which Jacqueline had rashly plunged. To be sure Gouda, Oudewater, Dordrecht, Zierikzee, and Schoonhoven had all refused homage to the new ruward and the Cods had been forced to withdraw from the latter city, so much was temporarily in Jacqueline's favour. But all the wealth of Burgundy was against her, besides her equivocal position in relation to the dukes of Brabant and of Gloucester.

Every effort of her adherents was exerted to put a force in the field strong enough to dislodge the ruward, while his foothold remained uncertain. Across the Channel, Humphrey had again awakened to interest in his wife's cause. His letters promised speedy aid, and he was no longer restrained by Parliament now that Jacqueline's fortunes seemed brighter.

Gouda became headquarters for the Hook

---

[1] *Tresorerie des chartes de la chambre des comptes de Flandre.* De Potter, p. 123.

camp and thither Jacqueline went, well escorted, after a feast had been offered her at Vianen. She proceeded to reassert her intermitted sovereign rights and despatched letters-patent to all the cities announcing her return to her own and asking their fidelity and support.

From his uneasy post at Paris, the Duke of Bedford watched these events in the Netherlands with great anxiety. With the wife whom Humphrey still recognised, though others contested her legal status, importuning him for aid, it was only too probable that he would again rush upon the scene, having gained some backing at home, precipitate hostilities with the Duke of Burgundy, force the latter to break his alliance with England, and for ever jeopardise the chance of the English retaining sovereignty in France against the pretentions of the Dauphin. Bedford decided to take immediate steps to prevent, at least, the scandal of the single combat between his brothers which had never been formally abandoned. To this end, he convened a solemn gathering at Paris. Bishops, royal officials, jurists, and heralds at arms were assembled. The two dukes were summoned to appear before this tribunal or court of chivalry. Both sent representatives, Humphrey, the Bishop of London, and Philip, a very clever diplo mat, the Bishop of Tournay.[1] These deputies were attended by privy councillors. All the voluminous letters exchanged be tween the two princes were brought forward, examined, and discussed for days. Doctors in both laws discussed the matter learnedly. The upshot[2] of the opinion of all these wise men was that honour did not require the duel. On his part Humphrey was right in his assertions, Philip, too, had a certain justice on his side, but princes should not risk their reputations and precious lives for the sake of an unfortunate word spoken in haste. Christian duty demanded that the two gentlemen should forget how they had wounded each other and should forgive each other in the presence of the assembly.

[1] Monstrelet, iv., ii., chap. 36; *Cartulaire,* iv., p. xlii.; Waurin, v., 195, etc.
[2] Given September 22, 1425.

The Englishman's friends declared that they thought he would accept this advice, but the Burgundian's envoys were positive that it was quite useless to carry such a message to their chief. They declared that he was now determined to meet his opponent and would not be deterred. With this assertion the question was left in abeyance, and as a matter of fact no duel was ever fought.[1]

In Holland and Zealand the situation was menacing. It was evident that the long party strife was about to be put to the test, —party strife into which foreign elements had now entered. Philip and Jacqueline were two striking figureheads, and around them as new centres, passions ran high. Hereditary hatred was added to new issues. Man was ready to fight man on the street, broils were incessant and occasionally grew into regular skirmishes, long before either claimant to authority was ready to pit his strength in a formal engagement.

At the end of September, 1425, Philip's

[1] According to Waurin, Philip went into training to prepare for this duel. The suit of armour he had made for the occasion was preserved at Lille for many years. *La Chronique,* v., lib. iii., chap. 41.

fleet appeared off the coast of Holland. There was an effort to prevent his landing, but the Hooks were too weak to be efficient. Philip was accompanied by some three thousand heavy armed men, besides other troops. At the outset he did not take the offensive, but prepared to make his progress in state, from one to another of the usual places of homage, as though his right of guardianship was unquestioned. In the majority of the cities he was received without protest, and his favours, scattered broadcast, won him many new adherents.

Jacqueline's party held a triangle of territory with the towns Schoonhoven, Oudewater, and Gouda at the apices. These towns were by no means the most important in Holland, but they were well fortified by water and dikes, and had good intercommunication with Utrecht, Amersfort, Muyden, and Naarden. There were plenty of open channels of communication with North Holland, Zealand, and North Brabant, where there was individual if not community attachment to Jacqueline, for even scattered through the districts where the majority held for Philip, were many who really preferred the Countess to a foreign duke. Zierikzee, Brill, and other Cod towns, all contained numerous sympathisers. Philip's material resources were, however, infinitely greater than his opponent could possibly furnish. Hook nobles might be willing enough to impoverish themselves in Jacqueline's cause, but even their all was insignificant. They were buoyed up by the constant hope that money and aid would come from England, but there was no guaranty of its fulfilment.

The Hooks were strong in single combat and in harrying warfare, and were clever in catching the lightest breeze of chance. Their greatest deficiency was that they had no leaders trained in even such military science as then existed. The men fought in little groups each close to his chief, and their loose ranks were easily broken by the firmer attack of the Burgundians. Plenty of mercenaries were at the service of any employer, but Jacqueline had an empty purse.

Moreover, she possessed no commander of a mettle to attract the roving bands who preferred serving under famous generals. Though there were a number of valiant noblemen in Jacqueline's camp, they were totally without the experience of such men as John of Luxemburg and others in the Burgundian service.

Six weeks passed after Burgundy had landed his forces, without an encounter between the foes. Then Philip began offensive measures in the region of Leyden. The strongest point held by the Hooks was the village of Alfen, up the Rhine about a league and a half from Leyden. Its situation was of peculiar strategic importance, inasmuch as it commanded the waterways in several di rections. Philip determined to make him self master of this place, where Jacqueline was herself in command. At his first onslaught the Hooks were repulsed, but they rallied and made a counter attack so unex pectedly that a sudden panic seized their opponents, who broke and fled, hotly pursued by the victorious Hooks. The latter actually succeeded in wresting the banners from the fugitives. With these flying and with other booty in full evidence Jacqueline and her little army marched triumphantly into Gouda, and the rejoicings over the good fortune were long and loud. In the great church of Gouda, a Te Deum was sung, while the banners of Haarlem, Leyden, and Am sterdam were displayed to the congregation. For years the flags remained on the walls of the church, and rarely would a burgher of the discomfited towns put foot within the edifice. As long as a city's banners were in hostile hands, similar ones could not be used at home. Philip hastened to send letters of condolence to the defeated cities—these were possibly some compensation for losses, as new support for the future was promised.[1]

For Jacqueline this victory of October 21st, small as were the numbers actually involved, was of great moment. That she, with her slender resources, had succeeded in repulsing the Cod party, backed as the

[1] Van Mieris, iv., p. 794.

forces were by the Burgundian power, gave her a sudden éclat. Many who had been doubtful in choosing sides, many who had thought that submission to Philip was wiser for the country's weal, now resolved not to desert their hereditary lady. The news that she was defying the Duke of Burgundy was carried over the Channel and quickened Humphrey to action. By mid-winter he succeeded by hook and by crook in raising a body of picked men, which he entrusted to the command of Lord Fitzwater. This time the Duke of Burgundy did not leave the duty of repulsing the expected attack to his subordinates. Informed that the English would land in Zealand, he hastened thither to meet them. He employed the interim before their coming in taking measures calculated to make the burghers feel that his friendship and his protection were advantageous. He confirmed all existing privileges, offered to repair the dikes, extended toll and staple rights, and made good interstate commercial arrangements.

Some cities continued to resist his authority, Zierikzee among them, but Dordrecht finally yielded and gave homage on November 11, 1425. The Duke took other precautions than military ones to woo success to his side, actually making pilgrimages on foot to certain chapels to beg the Virgin's intercession in his favour. A dire conflict was in store for him as all believed, and when a monstrous fish was caught off Zealand, its extraordinary size was deemed an ominous portent of great battles. From his head quarters at Leyden Philip kept a sharp outlook on the waterways for more than fish, and he succeeded in establishing a boycott against the wares of all cities which held to Jacqueline. The advent of the Duke of Gloucester with his English troops was now looked for eagerly by the Hooks. About Christmas time several gentlemen from Holland and Hainaut crossed over to London to beg him to make haste. Humphrey was not ready to come himself, but his lieutenant, Lord Fitzwater, with a force of three thousand, finally set sail. It was on January 4th, at two o'clock in the morning, that Philip of Burgundy was notified that the fleet was under way. He hastened to Rotterdam, where his own ships were in readiness, embarked, and dropped down the Maas. From all the cities which had offered homage, troops journeyed by land and water towards his standard.

Unfortunately for the invaders, the English boats drew too much water to reach the coast. Two ran aground and were seized. With lighter ships the allies might have gained Zierikzee before the gates were shut. Her burghers had declared that they were neutral before the battle. After it they would choose Burgundians or Englishmen according to the result of the day. Possibly with the English within their walls, they might have been led to an earlier choice. The invaders, however, succeeded in occupying Brouwershaven, a hamlet about six miles to the north of Zierikzee, whence they expelled the Cods who were within, and the village became the headquarters of the Hooks who flocked thither from all sides.

Jacqueline herself with her own troops did

not appear on the scene. A week passed, and then the allies decided to proceed to Gouda to unite with her before risking an encounter with the enemy. A portion of the fleet at once weighed anchor, but as the pilots were ignorant of the channel they encountered difficulties and their ships were grounded on the sandbanks. One of Philip's generals, Gaesbeck, instantly gathered a small squadron of light boats with slight draft manned with men who knew the channels. Watching for a favourable moment he sailed out of the back-waters and fell on the English boats caught like flies in a trap. They tried to fight on foot in the shallows but the sand gave way. There was no escape and the whole body were carried off to Biervliet as prisoners. Meanwhile Philip cruised about, fearing to engage in battle on account of the inclement weather, but making sure that no reinforcement from Jacqueline could come down the river. He also took the precaution of ordering that the Holy Sacrament should be carried through the streets of his faithful towns and that the blessing of God and His saints should be asked on the success of the Burgundians, and that this ceremony should be repeated daily while he was holding the English at bay. The delay was of great advantage to the neutral folk of Zierikzee, who provided both combatants with provisions and were well paid on each side.

It was a Saturday, January 13, 1426, when the storm cleared and Philip was able to bring his fleet into line of battle and proclaim his presence with trumpet, drum, and fife. The moment suited him and the English accepted his challenge. The men on land chose a fine vantage ground on top of a dike, where there was sufficient room for evolutions.

Well, the chroniclers tell a long story and elaborate the minor incidents of the conflict — the first instance of an actual encounter between the Burgundians and English, allies as they were.[1] Dynter and his echo, the

---

[1] Barante says that Fitzwater could not engage personally in the conflict as he had pledged himself never to fight against the Duke of Burgundy. If this were true he was a singular commander to despatch to Jacqueline's aid.

poet of the *Brabantsche Yeesten*, ignore Jacqueline's first triumph at Alfen, but they give plenty of space to this day when greater honour redounded to the Duke.[1] How could it be otherwise with all his resources and with the ground familiar to his Flemings, against a young, unskilled woman leader forced to depend for her every penny on the good will of her followers, whose numbers varied with the appearance of her success and with the uncertain winds from across the Channel? Nevertheless the struggle was a bitter one and the victory only won by a hair's breadth. At one moment all chance seemed over for the Burgundians. Philip himself seized his own standard and plunged into the thick of the fight to reanimate his men. He was so hard pressed that he would have perished had it not been for the timely aid of one Jean de Vilain. The Duke's words, "Whoever loves me, let him follow," just as all seemed lost, saved the day, according to Barante.

[1] Dynter, vi., cap. 222. *Brabantsche Yeesten*, vii., chap. 130. Monstrelet, Barante, etc.

The Burgundians were filled with wrath at having been so nearly defeated and wreaked their ire upon their captives in a sanguinary fashion. Very few of Jacqueline's own friends or of those sent over by her husband, survived the day. It was an overpowering calamity for her and the Hook party, while the Burgundian loss was also considerable for battles of that time. The actual injury was incalculably the heavier for Jacqueline's side, because it was suffered by burghers and countrymen fighting for their own cause on their own horses, not by hirelings to be replaced by their own kind, who made a living by risking their lives.

Appointing Roeland van Uutkerke his lieutenant in Holland, Philip remained in Zealand until that countship was satisfactorily reduced to his obedience. He was backed in his efforts by letters from John of Brabant desiring his loving subjects to obey his dear cousin of Burgundy as though it were himself.

It must be borne in mind that up to this point Philip was simply ruward and heir, not Count. The claim was that John of Brabant held in behalf of his wife and that he had ceded his authority for a certain period "for the sake of peace."[1] Philip's attitude, therefore, was that of guardian towards a rebellious child. John's letters were countersigned by various nobles, the Holland Count of Nassau, the Zealand Lord of Borselen, and others. One Borselen perished at Brouwershaven, but there were other members of this family and Frank van Borselen was a staunch supporter of the ruward. Zierikzee was the last town to submit. On March 15th the burghers gave homage and the ruward showed wisdom in granting them fairly lenient terms. Before Easter, Zealand was entirely under the control of Philip, and Jacqueline had lost all foothold among the islands.

[1] Van Mieris, iv., p. 817. In some authors twelve years is given, in others it is undetermined.

CHAPTER XI

The Countess Militant

1426–1428

SO Fortune answered the appeal to arms by allowing each cousin to carry off a decided victory. Then followed a dreary space of two years, when the active hostilities, defensive and offensive, inaugurated at Alfen and at Brouwershaven, dragged on in Holland, causing infinite misery within a small area of territory. There were a few sieges, a pitched battle occurred occasionally, but as a rule, petty, nagging, guerilla encounters succeeded each other. Divers municipal records preserve in their expense accounts stray and unconscious revelations of events passing during the contention for the overlordship.[1] There are items of fees

[1] Löher, *Beiträge,* p. 250. Burgundian writers give little space to these wars in Holland, but there are several Dutch chronicles, wherein they are discussed in detail worthy of greater events.

paid to women spies, dry statements of piteous petitions for reimbursement for forced contributions to both parties, and innumerable evidences of the utter wretchedness experienced within and without the city walls. Jacqueline and Philip alike were prodigal in their tempting bribes to communities and to individuals in order to secure their recognition, bribes in the form of advantageous chartered privileges, and of exemption from certain specified taxes.[1] The lady used her seal as lavishly as her guardian, but the latter backed his promises with a show of hard coin, while those of the penniless ward often remained empty words.

In her personal activity Jacqueline showed a tireless energy. She rode fearlessly into the field at the head of her own troops, and was in the midst of her faithful peasant friends in the siege of Haarlem. The chief advantage possessed by her was the devotion of the humbler folk to her cause. Their allegiance was unquestioned. In her service they were ready to furnish all aid and infor-

---

[1] Van Mieris, iv., p. 834 *et passim*.

JACQUELINE IN BATTLE.
XVIII century print.

mation possible. At Haarlem the chances in favour of the success of her investment were based on the hopes that the lower classes would revolt against the wealthy burghers, declared allies of Burgundy, and that a diversion would be created in favour of the besiegers. Such a sympathetic movement within, would have turned the scales to the advantage of the force without the walls. But the agitation was easily suppressed as an insignificant riot, and Haarlem held out. Jacqueline's most brilliant success was won on the same ground as her first, at Alfen.[1] Acting on intelligence afforded by a captured letter concealed deftly in bread, she surprised Jehan van Uutkerke, the stadtholder's son, and completely routed his Burgundian forces:

After this battle, as the story goes, the Countess knighted seven of her gallant gentlemen with her own hand. The scene is depicted in the frescoes at the Munich gallery, but its actual occurrence has been questioned, owing to the improbability of

---

[1] The anonymous history referred to as *The Hague Codex* contains a detailed description of this battle. Löher, *Beiträge*, p. 209.

the capacity of a woman to confer an honour she could not attain. The formal laws of chivalry prevailed at this time almost as much as when knighthood was in full flower. It is possible, therefore, that Jacqueline had to avail herself of the intermediary services of a duly qualified deputy to perform the rite *ex jussu dominæ*[1]

At her hand or at her behest, the recognition of spirited conduct by the bestowal of a dignity was a gracious act on Jacqueline's part. Other tales of her exercise of authority are less agreeable. Sometimes she forfeited friends by a want of tact, by undue severity, when leniency would have stood her in better stead. That last was a fault committed in her maiden campaign against her father's foes, and it may be that she repeated it at later stages in her career, when fact and fiction are so inextricably mingled in the stories recounted of her adventures that it is difficult to discriminate between them.

---

[1] Löher, *Beiträge*, p. 94, etc. One instance only is given of knighthood conferred by a woman before 1400. This was in the year 1111.

Not long after the battle of Alfen, when the glow of success still flushed the heart of the Countess, the following incident is said to have happened. One day a certain Jan Knuypf, of Hoorn, happened to be in Gouda on his own business, where he saw the young Countess in the midst of her soldiers, a position that seemed to him ill befitted to her sex and beauty. He said to a bystander, "It is a shame to drag such a beautiful noble lady around in camps, as though she were a vagrant." This remark was both casual and sympathetic, but the words were twisted and exaggerated in repetition until they sounded like a gross insult. Knuypf was suspected of being a Cod spy, as it was declared that no faithful Hook man would have spoken in such a manner of the sovereign lady. Arrested and tried for his offence, he was promptly condemned to death. At once his father, Lambert Knuypf, a well-to-do merchant, hastened from Hoorn and offered a heavy ransom for his son's life. This was refused and he was told that a summary example was necessary to protect the honour of the Countess. At length the father proposed that for the sake of a public example his son should be led to the scaffold, and then, just at the last moment, that Jacqueline herself should stay the executioner's hand at her own instance, and thus show mercy where the military necessities of the situation demanded severity. This petition was accorded to him—at least, he so understood it. But when the fatal moment came Jacqueline never lifted her hand, and the young man's head fell as a terrible expiation of his careless phrase. The infuriated and disappointed father declared that whatever happened elsewhere, in Hoorn the Countess should never be sovereign. Later, when she attempted to bring Hoorn to her allegiance, he was among the determined opponents who resisted her efforts. Moreover, he aided the cause by expending freely the sums he had collected for his son's ransom.

Arnold, or Allaert, Beylinck, the so-called Regulus of Holland, is another one whom tradition makes a victim to Jacqueline's determined severity. So firm was his resistance to her at Schoonhoven, that he was condemned to be buried alive, while the other captives were pardoned. Submitting to his sentence, Beylinck asked and obtained a week of respite and of freedom, to regulate his affairs. At the expiration of the time the reprieved man conscientiously returned and suffered the death penalty imposed upon him, a penalty ignominious in its nature, because usually reserved for women alone.[1]

Whether or not the resentment of the elder Knuypf was a factor in the decision of the Hoorn burghers, the town certainly declared for Philip, and Jacqueline's inability to reduce it by force weighed against her ultimate success.

During the progress of this unequal struggle, one natural protector to the weaker party might properly have been the Emperor. Sigismund, to be sure, had never recognised Jacqueline as rightful successor to her father, and had never withdrawn his own assertion

[1] Löher, *Beiträge*, p. 73. *Bijdragen, Vaderlandsche Geschiedenis*, new series, 6 and 7. Robert Fruin's conclusion is that Beylinck was executed but that Jacqueline had nothing to do with it.

that Holland and Zealand were male fiefs, even when his protégé, the ex-bishop, accepted a ruwardship instead of the count's title he first claimed. At the same time, as Philip's open intention was to erect a new realm for himself, and to sever it from the empire, it was hoped that Sigismund might be convinced that a weak ward would be preferable to the total disappearance of the shadow of imperial suzerainty. With a shadow there the substance might be renewed. But time proved that the Emperor was to have no weight in the balance. He neglected the opportunity of making his ancient rights felt indirectly. He was totally unable to sustain his own renewed claim put forward at various epochs after the death of John of Bavaria, and was troubled not at all about the injustice suffered by the hereditary princess, though he might have reaped substantial advantage by identifying himself with her cause.

English interest in the fate of the Duchess of Gloucester lagged after the defeat at Brouwershaven, where the loss had been so heavy. Numerous proofs exist to show the efforts of Bedford and Winchester to keep Humphrey from further embroiling himself with Burgundy.[1] Bedford left Paris and spent some months in England to watch his brother. Still, there are scattered evidences that the latter did not entirely abandon efforts to have the validity of his marriage settled. That he had legal advisers at work is shown in the following letter from William Paston to William Worstede and others. It is dated March 1, A.D. 1426.

"*A mes tres honnourés Meistres Will'm Worstede, John Langham, et Meistre Piers Shelton, soit donné*—[some business matters of his own]. I have, after the advys of your lettre, doon dewely examined the instrument by the wysest I coude fynde here and in especial by on Maister Robert Sutton a courtezane of the Court of Rome, the which is the chief and most chier man with my Lord of Gloucester, and his *matier in the said court for my lady his wyff:* and

---

[1] See discussions in the Privy Council about actual authority during the King's minority. *Proceedings*, iii., p. 237, etc.

their answere is that al this processe, though it were in dede proceeded as the instrument specifieth, is not suffisant in the laws of Holy Churche and that hem semyth by the sight of the instrument and by the defautes ye espied in the same and other and in maner by the knowlich of the notarie that the processe in gret part ther of is false and untrewe."[1]

During the first year of her active campaigns, Jacqueline found her sturdiest supporters in Kennemerland, the district stretching north of Haarlem where peasant proprietorship was in vogue. Here the people were full of sympathy for, and devoted to the cause of their hereditary sovereign and resented the pretensions of one who, to their mind, was a Frenchman pure and simple and alien to them. But their untrained efforts in her behalf were effectually crushed by the Burgundians, and the punishment meted out to them for their temerity was bitter and long enduring. The spring of 1427 found Philip occupied in de-

[1] *Paston Letters,* Gairdner's edition, i., p. 24.

termined efforts to root out the spirit of opposition to him, while Jacqueline was shut into Gouda with a diminished circle of adherents.

A new bull of sequestration issued by Martin V in 1426 also had some effect in chilling enthusiasm in her behalf,[1] when knowledge of it gradually spread abroad. This reiterated the statements that Jacqueline had violated all laws of duty and equity in deserting her husband, John of Brabant, and in robbing him of his dues; that she ought to return to him, but that the Pope would permit her to remain under the protection of her kinsman, Amadeus of Savoy, there to stay at her own expense until the supreme head of the Church pronounced final judgment on the suit. But there was no notion in her own mind of return to her abandoned husband. What were the hopes she continued to cherish, appears from a piteous letter written at Gouda on April 8th to the privy council of England.[2] It is one of the

[1] De Potter, p. 145. Original at Lille.
[2] *Cartulaire,* iv., p. 579. Original at Lille. See also *Beiträge,* p. 219.

many documents which followed each other to London. She says that in her person she is in excellent health, but otherwise in great care, fear, danger, and sadness, from which she implores the very high, very reverend fathers in God to release her. She reminds the young king that she held him in her arms at the font and that she was allied to him by marriage. She begs his advisers to urge her husband not to prolong her misery by futile messages and embassies which are her ruin,—but to "hasten to the safety of my seignories." This letter was despatched by Louis de Montfort and Arnold of Ghent, who are charged to tell more by word of mouth.

Scarcely had these trusty friends and counsellors crossed the Channel when all question of Jacqueline's return to her quondam husband-was settled for ever by his death.

Here is Dynter's account of the last illness of John of Brabant:

"In the year of our Lord, 1426, on Wednesday, April 9th, according to the style of the court of Cambray,[1] John, Duke of Brabant, and his brother, Count of St. Pol, travelled from Brussels to Lierre to the diet of the three Estates of Brabant. The diet being concluded, the Duke and his brother on Saturday, April 12th, after dinner rode toward Brussels. Between Vilvorde and Brussels, a severe illness seized him and it was with great difficulty that he reached Brussels at evening on the same day." The narration proceeds to say that the Duke grew steadily worse, until Holy Thursday, April 17th. He begged his brother to carry out the terms of his will, confessed, and received absolution. When these things were done he ordered Lord John of Rotselaer, Vorselaer, and Reth to wash and wipe the feet of thirteen poor persons in his behalf, and to give them food and money. " This order scarcely completed, pious Duke John, with his arms and hands crossed over his breast, began to read the psalm *Miserere mei Deus,* and before he could complete the first

---

[1] *Secundum stilum curie Cameracensis,* vi., cap. 226; Waurin, v., book iv., ch. 1.; *Beiträge,* p. 215.

verse he gave up the ghost."¹ Vinchant says that before his death John pardoned Jacqueline, *"pardonna tout le tort que la comtesse Jacqueline, sa femme luy pouvoit avoir fait."* It need hardly be said that Dynter, the official historian of Brabant, does more than justice to John's character and claims virtues for him not allowed by history. His poetical retainer, too, delares that the "many sweet words" spoken to him by his beloved lord are indelibly stamped upon his heart.² In spite of these eulogies, however, it is certain that John the Good was weak and vicious.

Yet his name is identified with one notable institution which reveres him as founder. From the year before his death dates the existence of the University of Louvain.³ The object of establishing this *studium generale* was to provide a place where scholars might acquire the learned professions at home in-

¹ Vinchant, iv., p. 111; Houart—*Historie ecclésiastique et profaine de Hainaut,* ii., p. 252—discredits the details of John's death as given by Dynter and others and is inclined to believe that he died from excess and dissipation. As usual in sudden death, poison was suspected.

² Author of *Brabantsche Yeesten,* vii., chap. 149.

³ Dynter, vi., cap. 223. See Papal Bull, Vinchant, vi., p. 164.

stead of wandering abroad to Paris and elsewhere. Several cities of Brabant declined the honour as they feared the unruliness of a student body. Louvain had lost prestige in manufacture and was glad to offer inducements to a new class of people to come to settle within its walls. Martin V accorded the same privileges to the new institution as were enjoyed by the universities of Padua, of Leipsic, and of Cologne.

CHAPTER XII

The Lost Cause

1428

AFTER the death of Jacqueline's titular husband, in whose name the Duke of Burgundy was acting as lieutenant, the question of the latter's status in Holland, Zealand, and Hainaut became complicated. Undaunted by the technical difficulties, however, Philip held his ground manfully, and declared that Jacqueline was a poor unprotected widow in her hereditary lands, and that he would kindly continue to administer affairs in her behalf.

In Hainaut he hastened to convene the Estates, and found great readiness on their part to entrust the administration of the government to him, the nearest kinsman of the hereditary lady. On June 22d and 23d he exchanged oaths with his new subjects and a charter was duly signed.¹ The ceremony of homage took place in the Church of St. Waltrude, where the young Countess of Hainaut had received fealty ten years previously.

This acceptance of her dearest foe did not pass without vehement opposition from Jacqueline and from her mother. The latter had continued her residence in Hainaut during the period of her daughter's adventures in the northern provinces. But the protests were unavailing, and most of them reached their destination after the decision had been practically concluded. The question was threshed out in a council meeting of May 12th. It was urged that Dame Jacque, heiress of these countries, had wrongfully married the Duke of Gloucester during the lifetime of her husband, John of Brabant. Further, that the said lady and the Duke of Gloucester were cousins in the

---

¹ He made various promises which bound him closer to the Cod party. *Cartulaire*, iv., pp. 589, 602 *et passim*. The charter is at Lille, with one hundred and seventy-two seals of clergy and nobles appended. *Beiträge*, p. 216.

fourth degree, and that in making him her heir she was setting aside her next of kin. For these and other valid reasons the Duke of Burgundy thought that "our said hereditary lady" ought not to be allowed to remain in possession of lands which she proposed to alienate, and for the "great good of the said country" he urged that he should be accepted without opposition. He mentioned that an answer could reach him conveniently at Valenciennes on the following Sunday. Philip knew how to ensure receiving a message to his liking, and the sequel has already been anticipated.

In Mons there was a strong sentiment against alienating the government definitely from Jacqueline. An assembly extraordinary was convened on May 27th to listen to her imploring letters and to resolve on the action of the capital city.[1] After deliberation, the voice of the majority declared in favour of accepting the protection of Philip, at least for the time being. He exercised infinite

[1] *Cartulaire,* iv., p. 593, etc.; *Beiträge,* ii., pp. 224, 227, etc.; Vinchant, pp. iv., 113, 114.

HENRY VI.
From a painting by Heath.

tact in winning over the people to his side, and there seems to have been a strong pressure of public opinion which affected official action.

Meanwhile Jacqueline's appeals to England were almost unceasing. In the act wherein Philip was recognised by the Estates as *Mambour* or governor of Hainaut and heir to the lady and princess, *dame Jacque de Bavier, duchesse et contesse des diz pais,* it is expressly stated that this condition is to last only until the lady disavows her marriage with the Duke of Gloucester [1] But in the epistles showered on King, on privy council, on Humphrey, and on Bedford, Jacqueline ostentatiously puts her English title first in her signature and evinces not the slightest inclination to abandon her position as member of the royal family. In a letter of May 7th,[2] she recapitulates her story, plaintively declaring that she went to England at the request of Henry V, and that he not

---

[1] *Cartulaire,* iv., p. 602. In all informal reference to her, "Duchess of Gloucester" seems to be the title used.

[2] Löher places this in 1427. *Beiträge,* p. 224. It would fit in better␣an earlier date, because there is so much reference to the stay at Ghent.

only promised her aid as a kinsman, but that as *specialis et pius pater* he pledged himself to give her paternal and faithful assistance in all her affairs. More than that she asserts that the late king, after taking the advice of his council, had himself betrothed her to his brother, the Duke of Gloucester.[1] In answer to a letter urging her to make a truce with the Duke of Burgundy, she responds, nominally, to Henry VI, with an emphatic statement that even to avoid the effusion of Christian blood she cannot now consent to make peace with the cousin "who counts on ousting me from my heritage." Passionately does she wish that the late king "had remained in human life," in which case "I know in truth that my affairs would not have come to the sorry state in which they are."

Ten days later she despatches her private secretary, Grenier, to the privy council with another letter. "I as a sorrowin

[1] " idem serenissimus rex . . . invocavit nobis futurum conthoralem præstantissimum suum fratrem, dominu nostrum ducem Gloucestrie." Löher says that the drafts of the Engli advices were often submitted to the Duke of Burgundy.

woman discomforted, left to endure miseries, to suffer the poverty and oppression which I have borne so long a time without aid or comfort, I recommend myself to your reverences," etc., etc Again she reiterates the terms of the express promise of the late good king. How hard, when after his death she had allied herself with his brother, that she should find herself "to-day despised and condemned by the whole world and like a *dame refusée* deprived of all comfort and counsel." She implores the gentlemen to urge her dear brother, the regent, and her lord and husband [no adjective of affection this time] to aid her. "Weary, grieving, I am left to wonder why God summoned my father to his company so early, leaving such a noble heritage to me, his daughter, once a happy child, and now condemned to lose my all through default of justice." Her near kinsmen are her deadly foes and she knows not which way to turn.[1] With this letter is a draft of what Jean Grenier is to say further to the council and the account he is

[1] *Beiträge,* pp. 227, 231.

to give of the events since the death of the Duke of Brabant, and of the arrogant pretensions of the Duke of Burgundy—how he insists that Jacqueline must disavow her legal marriage with Gloucester and renounce everything. Never on her life would she agree to such a treaty except by the advice of her lord duke and of the realm, unless indeed she were forced to it, was the burden of her argument.

There is a bitterer tone in this epistle than in former despatches. In her demands as to whether the English messenger who came to her in a very dilatory fashion, had really conscientiously represented her circumstances to the King, in her queries as to what Bedford and Burgundy discussed at their late meeting in Lille, and as to why no army is being levied for her, there is a note of despair and desolation, a note that, apparently, was not uttered in vain. For, on July 9, 1427, a decree was issued in the name of Henry VI, declaring that in consideration of the great troubles, dangers, adversities, and distresses which had been sustained by the Duchess of Gloucester,[1] "our very dear aunt," because of the affection borne her by the King, and on account of the numerous petitions made to the council by the Duke of Gloucester and by his said Duchess, and in virtue of the recommendation made by the Commons in the last Parliament at Westminster, he had decided to provide for the said Duke the amount of twenty thousand marks— namely: nine thousand by way of loan, five thousand "on account of said personal recommendation of our uncle," and four thousand out of eight thousand which he received yearly as protector of the realm during the absence of the Duke of Bedford, and two thousand from other sources;—the said sum was to be expended in the wages of men-at-arms to be sent into Holland to garrison the towns and places obedient to the said Duke and Duchess, and to escort the latter to England. No offensive operations were to be undertaken. The soldiers

[1] Rymer's *Fœdera*, x., p. 374; Van Mieris, iv., p. 894. *Proceedings of the Privy Council*, iii., pp. xlviii., 271.

remaining in garrison were not to attempt any further conquest in Holland, Zealand, or Hainaut, without the consent of the three estates of England. The loan of nine thousand marks was to be raised out of the subsidies and customs, from the revenues of the Duchy of Lancaster, and the profits arising from wardships and marriages. Articles were to be signed by the King and the Duke of Gloucester containing the covenants above specified.

But among the privy councillors themselves there is doubt as to the wisdom of this action. Two days later (July 11th) they write to the Duke of Bedford explaining that they were forced to it by public opinion, that the people declared that they could not answer to God, to the world, nor to the Lord and Lady of Gloucester, if they did not do all in their power to furnish her with aid in this dire crisis. They prayed Bedford straightway to ask his brother of Burgundy to redress Jacqueline's wrongs.[1]

[1] *Beiträge,* p. 236, etc.

How did Bedford answer this appeal? He concluded a truce with all possible rapidity and neglected no means of retaining his brother in England! He urged Humphrey, for God's sake, not to imperil his nephew's French kingdom. His strife with Philip was ardently desired by England's foes. He must give the minor king reckoning in the future if he injured him in his minority.

To the privy council, Bedford wrote on July 31st in still more urgent phrases. Philip was well inclined to peace and would gladly strike a truce for a year and a day if "the other party would but consent." He, Bedford, certainly could not think of asking Philip to abstain from war. It was plain that the question of the validity of Jacqueline's marriage rested with the Pope, and that of her heritage with the Emperor. In both cases was the English king free from all responsibility. Both were beyond his jurisdiction. The complaints of a sister-in-law must not be allowed "to imperil[1] the

---
[1] *Beiträge*, p. 240.

welfare of our kingdom." So anxious is the regent of France to reach the ear of the English council, that not only does he despatch this letter to the council collectively, but transcripts are sent post-haste to each of the councillors individually, as the council was not in session.

Four of Bedford's trusty gentlemen also hasten over the Channel to add verbal arguments to enforce his written words. All this was sufficient to stay, at least, the speedy despatch of the promised supplies for defensive operations, and Jacqueline continued her pathetic struggle on her own meagre resources. There was valour in her camp, but little else. Her faithful friend Brederode had succeeded in holding Texel against heavy odds. He had almost gained Wieringen when unfortunately he fell into Burgundian hands and was taken to Leyden, a prisoner. At this point, the approach of winter rendered actual fighting impossible. Philip withdrew to Flanders[1] and awaited the coming of spring.

[1] *Itinéraire de Philippe le bon. Col. de voyages etc.* Gachard, i., p. 79.

Meantime, another of Jacqueline's kinsmen had busied himself with her divorce suit, a kinsman upon whom, too, she had based some illusory hopes of support. Philip, Count of St. Pol, the new Duke of Brabant, now comes upon the scene. Out of respect to the memory of his late brother, he sends a fresh embassy to Rome. Who knows what other entreaties also found their way thither? In France there were waves of sentiment in favour of the uncrowned king at Bourges, the disinherited Dauphin The regent of Henry VI at Paris grew more and more uneasy, and probably both he and Philip intimated to their friends in Rome that nothing would please them better than a Papal sentence that would definitely deprive the Countess of Holland of any legal claim to English sympathy, a sympathy that was increasingly dangerous to France as an English dependency.

Martin V allowed himself to be persuaded. On January 9, 1428, the ultimate decision of the Papal court upon this *cause célèbre* was published. It is unequivocal in its terms. The validity of the marriage between John of Brabant and Jacqueline is reaffirmed and any other union contracted by the latter is declared null and void,—*nullius roboris vel momenti*.[1] Gloucester is not mentioned by name. Jacqueline's representatives in Rome immediately filed an appeal against this decision on the very day of its publication.[2] It was addressed to the Cardinal of Bologna and proved a futile attempt to stay proceedings. The parties pleased by the decision were strong enough to prevent any further tampering with it when once pronounced.

The intrigues of those months may be inferred. The difference in tone of Jacqueline's letters to Humphrey in 1425, and her references to him in those of two years later already quoted, is significant. She knew that he had no desire to return to Holland or to her The Duke had failed to join the wife whom he and all England recognised as legal Duchess of Gloucester, under the influence, not only of political considerations, but of

[1] Dynter, vi., cap. 231.   [2] Van Mieris, iv., p. 917.

HUMPHREY, DUKE OF GLOUCESTER.

the wiles and fascinations of another woman. From the hour when Humphrey had left Jacqueline in "our false and treacherous city of Mons," Eleanor Cobham had been his companion and mistress, and it is probable that she was encouraged by various persons in authority to exert all her charms to keep her lover at her side. Nay, it is said that she exerted other charms than her own. A certain Marjory Jordan, known as the witch of Eye, furnished her with a love potion which filled Humphrey's mind with thoughts of her and none other. Artificial means were, however, little needed. She evidently possessed adequate fascinations without employing magic arts. "Being a woman I will not be slack to play my part in Fortune's pageant" was a natural thought on her part at this stage in her career, as well as at the moment when the poet puts the words into her mouth.[1]

She was "a woman distinguished in her form," says Æneas Sylvius. "Eleanor, too, was beautiful and marvellously pleasant,"

[1] Shakespeare, *Henry VI*, Part II, Act I, sc. ii.

says Waurin.¹ The "too" (*aussi*) may refer to Jacqueline, who certainly may not have been "marvellously pleasant" when her affairs were going so drearily against her wish. Actual testimony is, to be sure, wanting to prove that Winchester and Bedford used Eleanor as a tool to work an end demanded by the exigencies of English foreign policy, but everything points to the suspicion that such was the case, and that the two were anxious to "buz these conjurations" in the brain of an ambitious woman, "knowing dame Eleanor's aspiring humour."²

When it was evident that Humphrey was released by the Papal decree from his contested marriage ties, it was perfectly natural that Eleanor Cobham should have been more than willing to intrigue in her own behalf to urge the Duke to give her his rank.

His delay in going to Jacqueline, the possible rumour of his intentions to accept his

---

¹ *Aleanor aussi etait belle et plaisante à merveilles.* Cronique, v. iii., chap. 37. *Beiträge*, p. 273. *Mulier ex militantibus forma præstans.* Æneas Sylvius.

² *Henry VI*, Part II, Act I, sc. ii.

divorce as final, aroused considerable indignation in London, and caused one notable effort in behalf of the deserted wife, if we may believe a strange story given in the records of the unknown monk of St. Albans.[1] He tells how a woman from the market, accompanied by several other women of London suitably dressed, publicly brought a petition to the Duke of Gloucester and other lords in Parliament. The tenor of this document was a complaint that the Duke did not deliver his wife from the durance in which she was held by the Duke of Burgundy, but, that with his love grown cold, he kept by him publicly a woman of ill fame, to the ruin of the realm and to the prejudice of the married state The monk or some one else inserts an incredulous *vacat* in the margin to show a disbelief in the report, even while he gives it for what it is worth. In Stow's hands the story becomes firmer. The market-place, *Stokkes*,[2] is metamorphosed into

---

[1] *Chronicon rerum gestarum*, etc., in Amundesham, i., p. 20.
[2] The market on the site of the present Mansion House was called hus from the stocks which stood there. See also Stubbs, *Constitutional Hist.*, iii., p. 106.

the name of the adventurous dame who led the petitioners:

"In this Parliament [1428] there was one Mistris Stokes with divers other stout women of London, of good reckoning, well apparrelled came openly to the upper Parliament and delivered letters to the Duke of Gloucester and to the Archbishops and to the other Lords there present containing matter of rebuke and sharpe reprehension of the Duke of Gloucester, because he would not deliver his wife Jacqueline out of her grievous imprisonment, being then helde prisoner by the Duke of Burgundy, suffering her to remaine so unkindly, and for his public keeping by him another adulteresse, contrary to the law of God and the honourable estate of matrimony : but what good successe their labours toke my Author reporteth not."[1]

If this petition were indeed presented it was as futile as the appeal at Rome and the

---

[1] *Annales, or a General Chronicle of England,* begun by John Stow, continued by . . . Edmund Howes, Gent., London, 1631, folio, p. 369. The marginal note is: "A crew of stout dames tries to check a great duke in open parliament." See also Southey, *Joan of Arc,* i.¹ p. 225; *Beiträge,* p. 276.

energetic market women might have spared themselves the trouble. The possible date of their effort is uncertain. As late as May 18th, the title of "our dear aunt Duchess of Gloucester" is applied to Jacqueline in a letter of safe conduct for her faithful adherent Arnold of Ghent, who is bringing her supplies.[1] In a document of June 10th it is omitted. It may be inferred that Humphrey's marriage to Eleanor Cobham took place after the petition, whenever that was, sometime after May 18th and before June 10, 1428. That a legal marriage was actually celebrated is, however, authentic, and undoubtedly this patently undesirable alliance for a prince of the blood, was furthered and sanctioned by his episcopal uncle and by his regent brother. The latter preferred a sister-in-law of doubtful reputation, to the risk of further embroglios with the Duke of Burgundy, whose friendship was becoming more and more necessary unless England were to lose for ever what had been gained by the Treaty of Troyes.

[1] Van Mieris, iv., p. 912.

Our author Waurin accompanied the Burgundian army when it returned to Gouda to complete the conquest.[1] This eye-witness comments on the fact that Jacqueline had succeeded in holding out so long at such terrible odds. But her power of endurance was finally at an end. The accumulation of misfortunes was overwhelming. There was pitifully little chance of any further success. The "grievous imprisonment" mentioned in "Mistress Stokes's" petition may refer to the fact that Jacqueline was pent up in Gouda, almost her very last stronghold. Everything combined to make her consent to a consideration of peace at any price.

The negotiations, opened at Bruges and continued at Delft, came to a rapid conclusion, and on June 29, 1428, Jacqueline, magnificently received in the latter city by her cousin Philip, signed a three weeks' truce. Four days later a treaty was concluded which comprised the following provisions[2]

1. Jacqueline must acknowledge her ac

---

[1] *Moi acteur de ceste œuvre estois en la compagnie de monseigneur l* Borgne etc. *Cronique*, v, lib. iv., chap. 3. [2] Van Mieris, iv., p. 91

quiescence in the Papal decision about the
legality of her marriage by notarial act.
She must withdraw her appeal made on
January 9th.

2. Philip of Burgundy recognised "his
dear cousin" Jacqueline of Bavaria as Countess of Hainaut, Holland, and Friesland, and
she acknowledged him as lawful heir and
present ruward or regent of the countships.
Both should again receive homage from
cities and nobles in their new rôles.

3. Philip should conduct the administration over the aforesaid provinces until Jacqueline married again with the consent of her
mother, of the Duke, and of the Estates of
her lands. If she married without the knowledge, counsel, and approval of the above
named, her subjects should be released from
all obedience to her or her husband and
henceforth should owe obedience only to
the Duke of Burgundy as ruward and heir.

4. As to the *aids,* two thirds should
henceforth serve for the settlement of old
debts, and the remaining third should be
divided between Philip and Jacqueline. The

remaining revenues, after the payment of official salaries and expenses, should belong to Jacqueline.

5. The fiefs of the countships were to be retained by Jacqueline. The fief lords must, however, also swear fidelity to Duke Philip.

6. Public affairs in Holland, Zealand, and Friesland were to be entrusted to a council of nine people, three nominated by Jacqueline, six by Philip, who should also appoint all officials in the countship of Hainaut.

7. The rival claims to the private estate of John of Bavaria should be settled by eight good men.

8. Exiles and refugees of both parties should be free to return and all injuries on both sides made good. All persons known to be implicated in the death of John of Bavaria were excepted from this provision.

9. There must be no further interchange of obnoxious party recrimination. The word "Hook" and "Cod" were to be spoken no more.

Such were the chief provisions of the treaty made to the honour of God, of His blessed

SEAL APPENDED TO TREATY OF DELFT.
July 3d, 1428.

mother, and of all saints male and female in heaven, and sworn to on the Holy Gospel by Philip of Burgundy and Jacqueline of Bavaria, by virtue of their Christian truth and princely honour

On the same day Jacqueline also signed a specific act recognising her cousin as heir in case of her death without children, which she did "to prevent any feud, contest, or war after our death to the ruin of our lands, people, and subjects." The original document is still at Lille. Jacqueline's seal attached to this act shows the Virgin holding the infant Jesus on her right arm and a palm branch in her left hand. A shield bearing Jacqueline's arms is supported by two lions rampant. The whole is enclosed in a hedge.[1]

Shortly after the settlement Jacqueline's mother arrived in Delft and confirmed the treaty on oath. It may be added that she then took the occasion to obtain new gifts from her daughter.

The proceedings were concluded by a joint progress made in great state by the

---
[1] Van Mieris, iv., p. 922.

late combatants from city to city. This began in mid-August. Every one swore to support Philip against all who infringed the rights ceded to him by Jacqueline. When affairs were established in Holland and Zealand according to the ruward's pleasure, he took measures to have his position confirmed anew in Hainaut. On Sunday, September 12th, the Duke and the Lady were formally received in Mons, and on the following day the Delft treaty was read aloud in St. Waltrude's Church. In her shadowy rôle of hereditary princess Jacqueline enjoyed the precedence in taking the oath and Philip followed in his capacity of affectionate guardian. This ceremonial was repeated in the other cities of Hainaut, and then the deposed Countess and her sovereign governor returned to Mons, where a gorgeous series of fêtes and tournaments were celebrated. In addition, there were hunting parties on a magnificent scale, "greater joy to the princess than to the peasants," over whose grounds the former rode. These lasted until midwinter.

Perhaps it was the magnificence displayed at these feasts of reconciliation that incited a certain Carmelite monk just then, to make attacks on luxury and eccentricities in dress to which fine ladies were addicted.[1] Especially severe was he on the pointed head dresses, and the noble ladies who thronged to his sermons were moved to abandon their finery and to appear in simple garb. "And God knows," says the Seigneur de St. Remy, commenting on the fine and stately festivities of which he was an eye-witness [2] "what joy the Duke and Duchess made together, and none would have suspected in what bitter warfare they had been engaged." It was an unswerving feature of Philip's policy to be conciliating when it was possible, and in all this recital it is evident that Jacqueline was well and honourably treated. It is difficult to reconcile her part in these gay scenes, where were present all the nobles who had fought against her party, with her own plaintive statements of her misery in her letters

[1] *Cartulaire*, v., p. 5, etc.   Monstrelet, iv., ii., chap. 53.
[2] *Chronique*, ii., ch. 156.

of a few months previous. There is no account of her own feelings, but there are abundant records to show how she used her dearly acquired income in pensions and rewards to the followers of her lost cause, and how she endeavoured to make good what they had risked in her behalf.[1]

[1] *Codex Dip.* (Hist. Genoot. te Utrecht 1852), p. 230.

CHAPTER XIII

The Silent Partner

1428-1433

PHILIP'S victory was thus pleasantly sealed with the kiss of friendship and Jacqueline had a plum, a cherry, and a fig in return for her provinces. To be sure, for a brief space, feudal supremacy seemed to be shared, not renounced, and supported by the administrative joint council of nine, wherein sat the representatives of hereditary countess and of present ruward. But only a few months elapsed before another adjustment was made. In a compact of January 24, 1429, Jacqueline compounded her share of the revenues for a fixed income of sixteen thousand crowns, the council of nine was abandoned, and Philip relieved his cousin of a still greater share of the burdens of life and of government.

It is touching to read in the preamble of the new treaty the reasons for the speedy change of base. The Duke was distressed that "our dear beloved sister" had not sufficient means from the uncertain income of the taxes to maintain her state. This conclusion was reached at about Christmas time when the two cousins met at Valenciennes,¹ and the formal document was signed a few weeks later. In addition to the pledged income, Philip assumed the responsibility for the repair of all the residences at Jacqueline's disposal. Her right to hunt where she would was expressly confirmed, together with certain feudal licenses, and the portraits of Duke and Countess were to appear on the coins.

The politic Philip continued his even and uniform system of treating his conquered foe with ostentatious legality and a brave show of courteous consideration, while he was edging her off her own ground with a

---

¹ Van Mieris, iv., p. 942. A series of documents pertaining to gifts and revenues were also signed at this time. *Cartulaire*, v., p. 61 *et seq.*; *Thes. rek.* p. 70 in the royal archives, quoted by Blok, *Bijdragen*, 1885, p. 319 etc.

succession of well directed shoves. He was full of cousinly love, was the good Duke of Burgundy, and he manifested his amity not only towards the Lady of Holland, but also towards his other childless relative, the Lord of Brabant, whom he honoured by a visit to Brussels in January where he enjoyed a series of fêtes, brilliant in spite of an untoward fall of snow and hail.[1]

With the spring he returned to France. This was the time when English sovereignty had received a rude shock, and his brother of Bedford was hard pressed to hold the French realm in behalf of his nephew. The troops levied for Jacqueline's service in 1428, had been taken by Salisbury to Orleans, which the English were preparing to besiege, to the consternation of the good burghers, who appealed to the Duke of Burgundy for aid to maintain a neutrality that had been promised them on account of the detention of their own Duke in England. It was at their request that Philip hastened to Paris in April. For a brief space he

[1] Monstrelet, iv. ii., chap. 54.

coquetted with both parties. The English regent felt that his brother-in-law's influence was of growing weight in turning the scale between English and French dominance, and exerted himself to retain his alliance. The persuasions of Bedford and his Duchess finally won the day and, though Philip's April visit was without result, when he again visited Paris in July there was a fresh crop of pledges of friendship with England, while his undying enmity towards the Dauphin, on account of his father's murder, was reaffirmed and proclaimed.

By that date, too, the siege of Orleans had been raised by the new leader who had suddenly appeared to espouse the cause of the uncrowned French King. Thus far the peasant girl was victorious against the same formidable alliance of opponents to which the princess had been forced to yield. What a pity it is that no record gives a hint of Jacqueline's opinion about Jeanne d'Arc! Probably she thought that actions meet for a sovereign defending her heritage were quite unmeet for the peasant, and probably too, she would have been no more complimentary in her adjectives than were the English about the arrogance of an untrained girl who dared enter the lists with men.

During the period of Jeanne d'Arc's ascendency in France, in the summer of 1429, Jacqueline remained in Hainaut, but in the following winter she took up her abode in Holland. Hainaut undoubtedly found it burdensome to maintain her state and was willing that she should carry it elsewhere.

In February, 1430, the Estates voted to give her six thousand pounds Tournois, to pay her travelling expenses to The Hague. On Monday, May 29th, the council at Mons listen to a report from three deputies on their return from an assembly of the Estates, where a discussion had taken place about assuming all the charges of the Countess. The question was decided in the negative.

From The Hague, Jacqueline despatches several letters about the beds she had established in the new Hospital St. Jacques at

Valenciennes, and on various other topics.¹ She provides in her "bouwerie" at The Hague for one Philip, the son of Claes, who has served her well; she makes a fine donation to Arent of Ghent, and lesser gifts to other faithful followers. Philip duly confirms these promises as well as other documents. A gift to a certain Jan Ruyschrock is interesting because it is a charge on the rent of the two Lombard houses at Zierikzee. If the tenants be behindhand, Jacqueline orders the schout and schepen to forbid the Lombards holding feasts, nay, more, they were to be restrained from trading within the city until the rent were forthcoming.

By the date of this last document, the Duke of Burgundy had removed Uutkerke from his office as stadtholder of Holland and Zealand, and put the Zealander, Frank van Borselen, in his stead, though under different and rather peculiar conditions. Frank van Borselen, of St. Martensdijk, and his two cousins, Philip of Cortgene, and John

¹ *Cartulaire*, v., preface, p. III., p. 110. Van Mieris, iv., p. 972 *et passim*.

of Soutberg, were not only entrusted with the administration of Holland and Zealand, but, in consideration of the payment of fifteen thousand crowns, they were to collect and enjoy the taxes. A commission was given to them for eight years, and an important article was inserted in the compact, expressly releasing them from the obligation of accounting for the details of their administration. Philip retained certain sovereign rights and Jacqueline, her titles. In November, Frank van Borselen assumed the designation of governor. He was in truth a farmer of the revenue and empowered to make as much as possible in order to reimburse himself for necessary expenditures.[1]

At this time Lord Frank was about forty, a well built, fine looking man, if we may trust the chroniclers—whose statements need many grains of salt. The Borselens

[1] "De Eerste Jaren der Bourgondische Heerschappij van Holland," 1428–1434 by Dr. P. J. Blok, *Bijdragen*, 1885, p. 327, Jacqueline's onfirmation of this appointment to "our dear true Lord Frank" is dated January 19, 1430, o. s. (1431). The cousins' names are given without endearing adjectives. There is no mention of the farmed revenues. *Codex Dip.*, 1852, p. 138.

were said to have descended from a noble family of Suabia. By the thirteenth century, however, they were established in Zealand and their estates were among the most important on those flat islands which offered none of the picturesque sites for mediæval castles afforded in German valleys.

Jacqueline possessed a hunting seat in Zealand,—Ostende, in the neighbourhood of Goes. This had been a favourite town of Count William VI. To him it owed its first charter, and his daughter had added to its municipal privileges when she received her first homage in 1417. In return, the town had presented her with a box containing six hundred gold pieces.

As the story goes, when the Countess was in residence at Ostende shortly after her abdication, she honoured the citizens of Goes by her presence at one of the archery festivals. More than that, she joined in a shooting match, hit the wooden parrot, won the prize amid admiring acclamations of the crowd, and was made queen of the day ac-

THE COUNTESS AT AN ARCHERY FESTIVAL.

cording to usage. Bilderdijk refers to this tale as a proof of Jacqueline's low tastes and unbecoming readiness to mix with vulgar sports[1]— hardly a fair interpretation of an act which also might be termed complaisant condescension on the part of a gracious lady wishing to be on friendly terms with her humble neighbours.

In memory of her success, she founded a new archery gild dedicated to St. George, — a strange choice! One might think that no saint in the calendar could be quite so distasteful to Jacqueline as the patron of Duke Humphrey of Gloucester. But possibly it was her father's predilection for St. George that she remembered.

It was during the hunting season when the Countess and Lord Frank were both in their Zealand homes that opportunity was afforded to the former to overcome her enmity to the Cod noble who had been so long in the field against her, and at last a valuable service rendered by Lord Frank bridged the chasm between the former foes.

[1] Bilderdijk, iv., p. 114.

One day it happened that the Dowager Margaret sent gifts of jewels and horses to Jacqueline, not by lackeys but by a goodly company of gentlemen, and, in accordance with the custom, it was obligatory for Jacqueline to give the messengers presents proportionate to the value of those they brought. The income arranged by Philip with the especial aim of enabling his dear cousin to live in due luxury apparently fell short of her needs. At this moment she had no money at her command and she could not let her mother's gentlemen go empty handed away.[1]

Secretly she despatched a message to the Lord of Montfort, her own former stadtholder of Holland, asking for a loan, but he answered that he had spent all he could afford in her service. This was unkind, because if rumour told the truth, he was still fairly rich, as he had appropriated much of the late Count's treasure and jewels. Her next appeal was to the Lord of Wassenaer, another Hook noble, who also refused her

[1] *Codex Tegernseer,* p. 26.

rather curtly. "Then," says Le Petit, "she went weeping to her chamber bewailing the ingratitude of her friends and servants and the shame of allowing her mother's people to depart with empty hands."[1]

Sympathising with her embarrassment, her faithful steward, William de Bye, suggested that it would be better to ask a loan from Lord Frank van Borselen rather than to confess poverty and fall short in the demands of courtesy. Lord Frank must have had a reputation both for wealth and for kindness, — or at least for being open hearted to women in distress, for there are records of large sums lent to Elizabeth of Gorlitz, the ex-bishop's widow, at an earlier date than this. The suggestion did not please Jacqueline. "He is a foe. We have wrought no good to him or his." De Bye urged her to overcome her reluctance and offered to negotiate the matter delicately. At last the poverty-stricken lady yielded to his persuasions. According to Le Petit, Bye then rode

[1] *La Grande Chronique*, i., 384. See also *Reygersberg Chron.*, art II., p. 200.

off to St. Martensdijk where he fulfilled the commission "mannerly and properly" — as well as successfully. "Carry this casket," said the noble lord, "to thy lady and bid her take therefrom what she needs. Tell her I ask this as a favour, and I shall count any future petitions from her as benefits to me."

How joyous was the faithful William de Bye to report this courtesy to his mistress! From that day on she regarded her ancient opponent and state officer with new and unofficial interest. When she was in Zealand, he invited her to visit his castle of St. Martensdijk, and she was graciously pleased to accept. Brave was the entertainment prepared for the lady. Throughout the castle the walls were hung with tapestries wonderful to behold. There was a red chamber wrought with angels, and another room where the hangings were embroidered with strange beasts. Rich bench coverings and cushions, a fine show of plate, and other luxuries gave evidences of Lord Frank's wealth and taste. But the chief mark of homage to his guest was displayed in the great entrance hall. Here the walls were decorated with garlands, into which the letter *D* was entwined, many times repeated. Lord Frank conducted his visitor from room to room, and was doubtless pleased at her pleasure and admiration. When she asked the significance of the *D's,* he bowed low, and told her that it was to signify his devotion to her service, to say to his lady—*Dijn williger dienaar.* He had not dared express his feelings with outspoken words.

Now the more confident and confidential chroniclers who love to lift the veil of history, declare that Jacqueline was so touched by this respectful and delicately offered affection that she was led to forget at last the desertion of the fickle Humphrey and all her other woes, and to accept the ardent and humbly proffered love of the Zealand noble. The difference in rank between the two does not appear abysmal across this distance of time. He was a noble of high degree and position and withal evidently possessed of unusual wealth. She was the dispossessed sovereign lady of three tiny countships, tossed and buffeted by harsh winds of adverse fate. Her quondam sister-in-law Catherine of Valois, widow of Henry V, stooped to wed a simple Welsh gentleman. Far more discrepancy seemed to exist between a daughter of France, widow and mother of an English king, and Owen Tudor, than between Jacqueline and Frank van Borselen. It was, therefore, probably not the difference in rank that made Jacqueline fear to announce her intentions of contracting a new alliance, and that led her to break her pledge of the Delft treaty, and to marry Lord Frank privately in her own apartments at The Hague, as the chroniclers say that she did, "With certain people as mediators," adds the author of the *Codex Tegernseer* in his narrative.[1]

That writer proceeds to tell how Philip was in Paris when news was brought him of this high handed and secret act on the part of his lieutenant and ward. Losing no

[1] *Viris mediantibus aliquibus.* The *Codex* brings Philip to The Hague in July and concludes the story of the loan with the secret marriage.

time, the Duke hastened to The Hague accompanied by his wife, Isabel of Portugal, with an escort of six hundred archers, who might be put to other uses than to serve as a guard of honour to the Duchess of Burgundy. At first there was no intimation that this visit had other significance than cousinly regard combined with Philip's natural desire to inspect affairs in his acquired territories. There was reason enough for his presence, and possibly Jacqueline disguised her fears that anything might be discovered, and that danger menaced her and her newly wedded husband. Some days, perhaps weeks, passed before the bomb burst in the sudden arrest of Lord Frank. One night,—it was November 25th,—Lord Philip de Ternant, a young and devoted follower of Duke Philip, lay in wait for Borselen as he returned from escorting the Duke to his apartments, declared him his prisoner, and conducted him to a little boat lying in readiness close under the castle wall. Borselen was carried to Rotterdam, where a ship was waiting to take the captive farther, to the stronghold of Rupelmonde in Flanders.[1]

When Philip found proofs that the reported marriage between his stadtholder and the titular countess was a fact, he considered that he had been basely betrayed. A messenger was despatched to Rupelmonde with a warrant for Lord Frank's death. The prisoner was discovered playing chess with the castellan. The latter took the letter from the hand of the courier, read the warrant, and turned to the board to continue the game as though there were nothing significant in the message. In spite of his efforts to be nonchalant, his change of countenance, was, however, too marked to pass unheeded by his opponent, who insisted on knowing the purport of the paper. "So at last my foes have overcome the Duke's goodness," was the latter's comment.

At his own suggestion, Lord Frank was

[1] The *Codex* says that Lord Frank was taken off secretly in a boat to Rupelmonde, and that the Count de Meurs liberated him with great difficulty upon the condition of Jacqueline's resignation. There are many slightly differing versions of the story.

See also, " De Eerste Jaren," etc., Blok.

hidden away by the friendly castellan, who then informed the Duke that his behest was obeyed. Philip's speedy repentance and genuine sorrow at the execution of his will led to a confession of the ruse, and to an accommodation of affairs. Such is one story.[1] Another is that Jacqueline, stricken with grief, made ready a fleet and sailed down the Scheldt to rescue her husband. Philip was at Rupelmonde before her. Before she had an interview with her cousin, Jacqueline asked to be assured that the prisoner was still in life. He was suffered to appear at an open window, where she could see him from the deck of the ship, where she stood watching eagerly. Once convinced that he was unharmed, she hastened to Philip's presence and declared herself ready to accede to his utmost demands, provided only that her husband might be forgiven and released. The penalty exacted was the final and complete renunciation of her heritage, her abdication from the last vestiges of sovereignty as expressed in her titles. One

[1] See Löher, ii., p. 492 *et seq.*

English chronicler, Edward Grimeston,[1] adds to this story of Jacqueline's sacrifice in behalf of her husband, the dark suggestion that, after his imprisonment, Borselen was a broken man as a result of an enervating drink given him at Philip's command to ensure a failure of heirs. But these extra touches only appear in narratives that have had time to gather moss through the rolling years, before they were written down

Later investigators into the actual facts of the case scoff at the idea of love passages between Jacqueline and Lord Frank, both no longer in their first youth. They clothe the bare skeleton of well attested data with a different substance of conclusions, and their treatment of the story must now be considered

During those years between 1428 and 1433, Philip of Burgundy had every reason to be pleased with life. His desires were bearing fruit. In 1421, the inpecunious and debt-burdened John III, Count of Namur, had sold his countship to Philip for a round

[1] *A Generall Historie of the Netherlands*, p. 54, London, 1627.

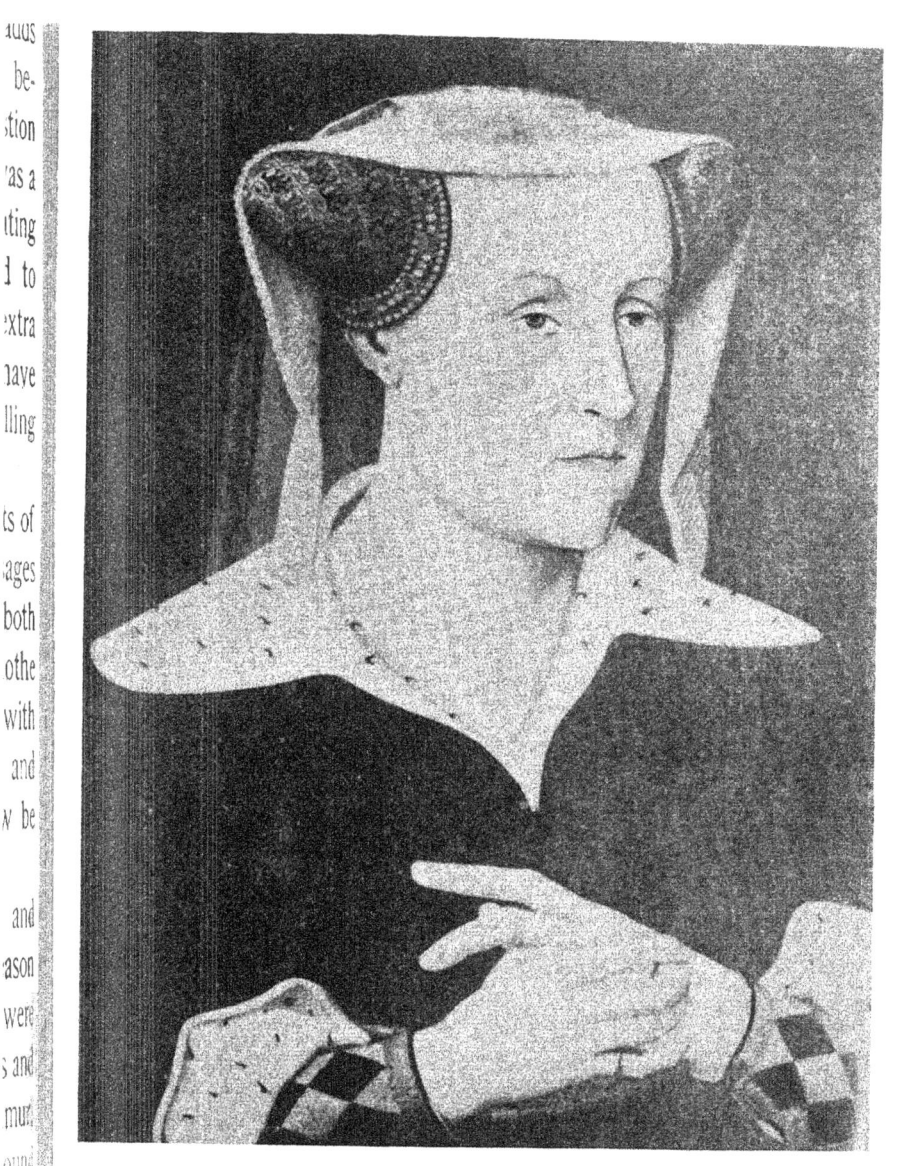

PORTRAIT OF JACQUELINE. 1431 (?).
Copy of original by Jan van Eyck. In the Royal Gallery, Copenhagen.

The Silent Partner

cash sum of one hundred and thirty-two thousand gold crowns, with the proviso that the sale should not be concluded until his death. On March 1, 1429, John III died. There were no direct heirs to dispute his right of disposing of his petty sovereignty, and Philip of Burgundy was acknowledged his successor without serious opposition. In the following year (August 4, 1430) a still larger and richer plum fell into Philip's hands on the death of the Duke of Brabant, exhausted like his late brother John at an early age from excesses and dissipations.

Here the succession was disputed. The Dowager Countess of Holland, Jacqueline's mother, was one degree nearer the late duke than her nephew of Burgundy. As Brabant had originally come to the Burgundian branch of the Valois family through a woman, her claim was not unprecedented. But Philip had not a mind to be troubled by the hobgoblin of consistency, and he paid as little attention to futile clamours as to feeble imperial assertions that Brabant was a lapsed fief. Only a few weeks prior to this event, Philip had declared that all the flotsam and jetsam cast up by the sea at Noordwijk should belong to his dear Aunt Margaret[1] and to none other, but when sovereignty was in question affection could be easily set aside and he ignored her claims.

Thus was the circle of his territory expanding. The state that he maintained was magnificent and he gathered adherents about him in a right royal fashion. When his nuptials with his third wife, Isabel of Portugal, were celebrated at Bruges in 1430, Philip instituted the Order of the Golden Fleece, and bound his chief nobles to him by a further tie.[2] Still on his side, he never forgot that in one slice of the territory he controlled he was not yet sovereign, only heir to the Countess. Holland, Zealand, and Hainaut had welcomēd him as ruward simply because they longed for peace and for the protection of a strong hand. But it is possible

[1] July 11, 1430, Van Mieris, p. 982. Possibly this is a direct bargain because three days later the dowager releases the people of Krimpenerwaard from all sea and dike service due to her.

[2] Vinchant, vi., p. 174.

that within a few months after his acceptance, these same territories had repented their action, and felt the inconvenience of an absentee overlord with his fingers in many foreign affairs, his interests involved with England and France, and he himself French to the backbone and far more concerned with Netherland revenues than with Netherland interests.

The financial arrangement with the Borselens did not run smoothly. As farmers they could not raise the estimated amount. It was difficult to pay the income of sixteen thousand crowns pledged to Jacqueline, while in addition to that, various specified revenues were weighted with charges of divers kinds. Again, taxes which might have been collected easily by agents of the all-powerful duke were refused or wrangled over when assessed by the farmer, who could not so easily enforce his claims. The death of one of the three Borselens, Philip of Cortgene, in 1431, brought about some complications in the settlement of his estate, and Lord Frank was summoned to Ghent in January of 1432. Here we find Isabel acting in behalf of her husband. In June, the governors accompanied by Boudijn van Zwieten go to Brussels where they see Philip in person, but the items of their discussion do not appear. It is only evident that there is much dissatisfaction abroad. Now it is very probable that, during the summer, the two ancient factions of Hooks and Cods which had so long been inimical to each other evinced a disposition to coalesce in joint hostility against Philip.

Jacqueline's mother, ill-content with chance flotsam and jetsam tossed up by the sea on the Noordwijk shore, as a compensation for the riches of Brabant, was implicated in one dark plot against the Duke's life which was discovered in the summer of 1432. Ægidius Postelles and a follower were arrested at Margaret's little court of Quesnoy and paid for their share in this project with their heads. Now if disaffection against Burgundy thus found expression in Hainaut, an alliance between the dispossessed Countess and a noble like

The Silent Partner

Frank van Borselen, the head of the latent Cod party in Holland, might be still more significant as an evidence of aroused nationalism against foreign domination. A similar union had been the dream of William VI on his death-bed, and what more natural than that some one should recall the dream now, when neither faction was in arrogant enjoyment of power? Again, that summer was a period when the bonds between England and Burgundy were loosening. Consequently it is not improbable that England was looking for commercial friendship in the disaffected Netherlands. Instead of overwhelming passion that swept away all other considerations, political motives may well have suggested the advantage of a bond between the heads of the Netherland parties, whose very names were condemned to oblivion. Such was Philip's fear — revived pretensions on the part of the hereditary Countess supported by Cods as well as by Hooks. The phrase used in the *Codex Tegernseer* suggests something like united action. Monstrelet speaks only of a rumour of an intended marriage.¹ When the ducal party and their six hundred archers arrived in The Hague, Lord Frank was absent in Egmont. What really happened before Lord Frank was dismissed from his office on November 1st, does not clearly appear. The accounts give the day of his arrest as St. Catherine's Day, November 25th. But it was no sudden and dramatic action as the chroniclers would have us believe. Here again the accounts are communicative.² Messenger fees paid November 20th show that Philip had sent letters to the cities to inform them formally of his arrival and of Lord Frank's projected arrest before it took place.

By December 1st, Philip was certainly again in Flanders, and may have been at Rupelmonde as the stories relate.

No romantic reasons are hinted at in the sober document finally signed on April 12,

---

¹ In the *Kroniek van Gouda* and in Monstrelet, both contemporaneous, there is no suggestion of a secret marriage.

² *Rek.* (1432–33), p. 50. *St. Katharinendach doe her Vrancke gevangen wart.* See "De Eerste Jaren," etc. *Bijdragen,* 1885, p. 333.

1433, at The Hague. We can only infer that it culminated some series of events tragic enough to bring Jacqueline to her knees before her cousin. She, the Amazon used to battles and to camp life, confesses that she is "a feminine person" and conscious that she cannot command obedience, nor administer government in peace, rest, and tranquillity.[1] From these and other reasons pertaining to the commercial interests of her subjects she decides that no one is so perfectly able to render them good service as "our dear brother of Burgundy," whose lands lie all around. That same brother is "our true heir and next blood." Accordingly "out of perfect love and natural affection, without the least compulsion and beyond the power of revocation on our part or on the part of our descendants, we give and bestow all the powers of sovereignty, high and low, territories, cities, castles, and peoples of the countships of Hainaut, Holland, Zealand, and Friesland, together with the garrisons, rights and liberties, revenues, aids, etc.,

[1] Van Mieris, iv., pp. 1012-1015. *Eene vroulijcke persoen.*

marches, gifts from ecclesiastical estates, etc. —without reservation of anything that has accrued to us from our father, Duke William, and uncle, Duke John of Bavaria, of blessed memory," etc. She was to release all her subjects from their oaths and to enter into no bonds with Philip's foes. Freedom of chase was, however, especially reserved to Jacqueline wherever she might please to hunt in her former domains and in all Burgundian territories.

Eight columns of Van Mieris's great folio are filled with the arrangements between this humble "feminine person," this poor weak woman conscious of her incapacity, and her powerful rival.[1] It is easy to pick flaws in the accuracy of the chroniclers, who copied carelessly one from the other, without duly weighing the value of what they quarried, but they are truth personified as compared to the legal documents cumbered with phrases designed expressly to conceal thoughts.

[1] There were two copies in Dutch and two in French. One of each is at Lille. For the French see *Cartulaire*, v., p. 177.

Estates were duly provided for Jacqueline, —the islands of East and West Voorne and the city of Brill, South Beveland, Vere, and various other places in North Holland and Friesland, while others were to fall to her after her mother's death. And, most important of all, in addition to certain other specified tolls, Jacqueline was assured five hundred "clinquars"[1] annually from the revenues of the countship of Ostrevant. All further claims were settled by a lump sum of one thousand pounds Flemish. There were certain limitations set to Philip's power of government, but henceforth he was free to style himself not Ruward but Count of Holland, Zealand, and Hainaut, and Lord of Friesland.

His cousin's title was to be henceforth Jacqueline, Duchess in Bavaria, of Holland, Countess of Ostrevant.[2] This last was significant. For some generations it had been the title of the next heir to the countship.

---

[1] Burgundian crown pieces. One of Philip's first acts in Hainaut was to regulate the currency, which was in a confused state from the variety of coins in circulation. *Cartulaire*, v., pp. 184, 188, 212.

[2] *Jacque Duchesse en Bavière, de Hollande, Comtesse d'Ostrevant.*

Thus Jacqueline and Philip completely reversed their relations to each other. The heritage was to return to her and to her descendants in case of failure of heirs in the Duke's direct line. Now Philip had no children from his first two marriages and had already lost two infant sons borne by Isabel of Portugal. Thus this provision gave some promise of restoration to Jacqueline and her heirs. But in all the verbose phrases of this document, there is no hint of Jacqueline's immediate intention to marry. Nor is there the slightest suggestion that it was an already existing marriage tie formed in direct violation of her positive pledge to Philip, that justified him in confiscating all the rights secured to his cousin on her abdication.

Only here and there do records and chronicles agree. An order to the castellan of Gorcum[1] forbidding him to yield up the castle as "long as Lord Frank is imprisoned" settles beyond question the fact of Borselen's imprisonment there.

[1] *Bijdragen*, 1885, p. 340. *So lange as her Vrancke gevange lach*

LORD FRANK VAN BORSELEN.
In the National Gallery, Amsterdam. Circa 1436.

In March, Philip returned to Holland and sent messages of summons to the cities, whose deputies convened in answer to his demand on April 3d. Nine days later the final treaty was signed. A certain number of pensions paid from May for "good offices rendered" show a list of Cod and Hook nobles. If there had been a national movement of rebellion against him, Philip assuredly displayed masterly skill in suppressing it, and the rest of his procedure was in keeping with his usual policy. It was stipulated in the treaty, because "we Duke and Duchess are both present in Holland" that together they should visit the cities, and the ex-Countess should formally release her subjects from their obedience to her. This was done, and again with great show of amity, Philip and Jacqueline made a slow progress from city to city, so that all her world could see how she acquiesced in her deposition from Countess of Holland to Countess of Ostrevant. In Hainaut and Zealand it was stipulated that the release of the people was to be made by brief, "in case we cannot go thither with our said brother."[1]

Hugo van Lannoy, a Hainauter and thus neutral to both Holland factions, was appointed stadtholder of Holland and Zealand. The eight-year compact between Philip and the Borselens was not honoured by mention even in the breaking of it. But a new compact was made on April 20th, wherein a pension of three hundred Burgundian crowns is settled on Lord Frank, either by way of compensation for his imprisonment, or as a bribe to renounce claims to the heritage of his wife or bride. By June 27th, the Zealander was reinstated in freedom if not in office, for messengers summon him to a new diet at Leyden.[2]

Thus did the Netherlands pass over to the House of Burgundy and become subordinated for one hundred and fifty years to government administered from abroad or by stadtholders.

Philip does not rest content with pro-

[1] *Cartulaire*, v., p. 190 *et passim*. Jacqueline dates her letters from Valenciennes on May 12th, but possibly Philip was not with her.
[2] "Bodeloonen," June 25, 1433; *Bijdragen*, 1885, p. 343.

clamations and statements published on the spot explanatory of the fashion in which all has passed, and of Jacqueline's satisfaction that "our dear brother" is about to secure peace and commercial activity for her people which she, "a feminine person," had failed to attain. To the King of France, to the Pope, and to the Council at Bâle, the Countess proceeds to despatch letters over her own signature, but evidently compiled with the neatly turned Burgundian phrases of the treaty, wherein she tells her own news of her resignation with never a word of her marriage,[1] nor of the fact that the open treaty of April 12th was not the only document signed on that day. There was also a secret compact, wherein it was provided that Jacqueline might marry a gentleman from the neighbouring territories under condition of the approval of Philip's councillors.[2] In the commission given to them the terms of the secret treaty are referred to and the reasons for the present action are

[1] *Cartulaire*, v., p. 203, *et passim*.
[2] *Bijdragen*, 1885, p. 343. Prof. Blok's reference is *Van Limb. Brouwer, Bourg. ch. 12 April, 1433.*

recapitulated. But it is not only by virtue of compacts that the beneficent duke acts. He alone is the natural protector of his cousin. He is bound to guard her honour and it is from his marvellous affection and ever loving concern for her welfare that he sends his own chamberlain and treasurer to assist her with their advice upon her projected marriage. On December 9th, Anthony de Croy and Guy Guilbant were accordingly appointed by Philip to take the matter into consideration.[1]

January 27, 1434, is the date of the document wherein these worthy gentlemen give their sanction to what probably had taken place eighteen months previously. The whole method of procedure is curiously roundabout. It seems as though Philip wished to keep in the background while justifying his position to the world. The articles of marriage are finally signed on March 1st[2]· "Jacoba, Duchess in Bavaria, Countess of Ostrevant, is empowered to marry with the

[1] Van Mieris, iv., pp. 1028, 1029.
[2] *Ibid.*, p. 1032. The titles of Jacqueline's new estates are also used.

noble and powerful knight Lord Frank of Borselen, Seigneur of Zuilen, of St. Martensdijk, and of Cortgene and with no other." Both parties shall incur no blame or reproach from my lord the Duke. Both parties are freed from debts contracted by the other before marriage In case of Jacqueline's death without heirs, Lord Frank pledges himself to swear off all claims to her heritage at large, but there was some property which she was free to bequeath, and she assures him a pension of twelve thousand Burgundian *schilde*.

When Philip gives his own sanction (June, 1434) to the alliance approved by his deputies, he goes a step farther, and raises Lord Frank to the dignity of Count of Ostrevant, while according him acknowledged relationship as "our dear cousin." His own goal was attained, and he could afford to be lavish with meaningless courtesies and to permit his crushed rival's husband to rank with princelings.

The public rite of marriage was at last performed in the chapel at St. Martensdijk, in that very castle of Lord Frank's where tradition gives the fête distinguished by the twisted *D's*. If the impetus to this union sprang from the hope of regaining the provinces for their posterity if not for themselves, it was, like many of Jacqueline's desires, doomed to disappointment. She had no children and was herself soon cut off from presumptive heirship by her cousin's better fortune. By the time the title of Count of Ostrevant was granted to Lord Frank and succession was secured to his family in case of default of ducal heirs, Philip's own son Charles[1] was more than a year old, and had proved a sturdier baby than his two infant brothers who came into life only to leave it. The Duke's long cherished schemes of founding a dynasty were therefore more assured, and he could afford to be generous in promises, based on unlikely conditions, thrown to the woman to whom his last gifts were the office of supervising the woodlands in her ancient domain and the title of Lady Forester.

[1] Born in 1433, he succeeded his father in 1467, and was known as Charles the Bold.

CHAPTER XIV

Lady Forester

1433-1436

DIVESTED of the few shreds of the phantom sovereignty first accorded to her, Jacqueline seems to have settled down to the kind of existence led by any noble châtelaine within her own domain and to have enjoyed the various pleasures to be found upon the estates at St. Martensdijk, at The Hague, and at Teylingen. This last was a hunting seat in the Haarlem woods, where the newly created " Count of Ostrevant " and his wife resided for part of the year, and where first she, and then he, exercised authority as Forester of Holland.

Two legends sprang into being about our heroine's ways of life in this particular dwelling, originating from the discovery in the moat of a number of small earthenware jugs, known as *Vrouw Jacoba's kannetjes,* or *kruitjes,*—Madam Jacoba's mugs or jugs. One theory was that Jacqueline devoted her leisure to pottery making, and that these little vessels, identified with her name, were turned off from her own wheel in the years after Fortune's wheel had turned her strenuous days into a series of undisturbed hours. One English writer sagely suggests that in this peaceful occupation the former Countess of Holland not only gave an impetus to an excellent home industry, but also introduced a new word, taken from her husband's name, into her native tongue, which has passed into English in almost identical form.[1] From "Borselen" this ingenious antiquary derives *porselein,* porcelain, an etymology which is as harmless as the tradition. At least it casts no slur on the memory of the defeated Amazon, even though she herself might have preferred

---

[1] *Journal of the Archæological Association,* vol. xxvii., 1871, p. 218. "Episodes in the Career of Humphrey of Gloucester and his first Duchess." It would be difficult to find more errors to a page than occur in this article.

another kind of a reputation than that of a Holland dame devoted to domestic arts.

The second story is less friendly, for it accuses "Vrouw Jacoba" of having emptied her own *kannetjes* of wine, animated by a desire to drown in oblivion the recollections of her chequered past. Bilderdijk paints the ex-sovereign as spending the days of her retirement in mad carouses, a fitting termination, as he implies, to her unwomanly military escapades.[1]

The one explanation is as little true as the other. The cups were used at Teylingen, emptied probably at Jacqueline's own table, but many shared in the task, and the numbers found may be accounted for by the custom of tossing away the beaker after it had been drained with a toast to a person or to a lofty sentiment. Never again was it to be put to commoner usage. Undoubtedly there were feasts in plenty at Teylingen. It was situated in the midst of the wooded district, where Jacqueline and

[1] His theory is that a euphemistic phrase signifying inordinate drinking, *het legen van kannetjens*, was the seed of both the above legends. *Vaderlandsche Geschiedenis*, iv., p. 123. *De Dichtwerken*, xiv., p. 17.

Lord Frank enjoyed the pleasures of the chase, an amusement essentially social in its nature. As a matter of course, the Lady Forester would entertain the hunters, and her merry and devoted guests tossed off many a draught to her health and to poetical thoughts or *spruchs,* and then paved the moat with the *kannetjes* that have been piled up into a monument to the châtelaine's discredit, or to point her descent from her proud ambitions.

Now that everything was bent to his will, Philip took care that his cousin should be amply supplied with money and enabled to maintain a certain state. Minstrels thronged her petty court as in the early Hainaut days. Music was a diversion next in favour to outdoor sports, as is shown by various receipts Jacqueline's rooms, too, were luxurious in such elegance as the age afforded, though they lacked many a comfort known to Holland burghers within a few decades of this period, still on the edge of the Middle Ages. Hangings and tapestries abounded and were well preserved as is testified by bills for cleaning and repairs. As for her own apparel, Jacqueline, even as Lady Forester, possessed almost as many gowns as Queen Elizabeth. Robes of gold cloth, plain and fur-edged, of damask, silk, and sober weaves, garments of various hues and of a wondrous variety of patterns, and headgear to match, were found in her chests. Traces of economy are apparent here and there, two pairs of sleeves, for instance, serve to a single dress. Also Dame Jaque was saving, for many of her belongings were too much worn to be utilised by any one, when they were exposed to public gaze after she had finally discarded them. But on the whole, her wardrobe was rich and costly.

Her jewel-box likewise was well stocked with various ornaments and many chains. Some of these were studded with jewels of price. In one, for example, there were fourteen sapphires and one hundred and eighty-nine pearls, while other necklaces were less brilliant but valuable. Strange that so large a store of gold chains survived the hard-pressed years of warfare. At that time and for at least a century after, chains similar to these were used like purses of coin, spent out link by link, to settle a bill at an inn or to satisfy the clamours of troops.

Less able to indulge in æsthetic tastes or to stimulate learning than her uncle of Bavaria, or the dukes of Brabant and of Gloucester, or her lavish cousin of Burgundy, it was only possible for Jacqueline to be a patron of art and letters in a small way.

It was a period when artists looked for a Mæcenas able to help them on their way, as well as sufficiently cultivated to appreciate their work. Jan van Eyck deserted Holland for Flanders even before the death of his first patron because the Duke of Burgundy lured him to Ghent with advantageous offers. The best craftsmen laboured for the highest bidder. Jacqueline had much less to attract talent to her service than her father or her uncle, and among the friends and followers mentioned by name in her will is neither poet nor painter.

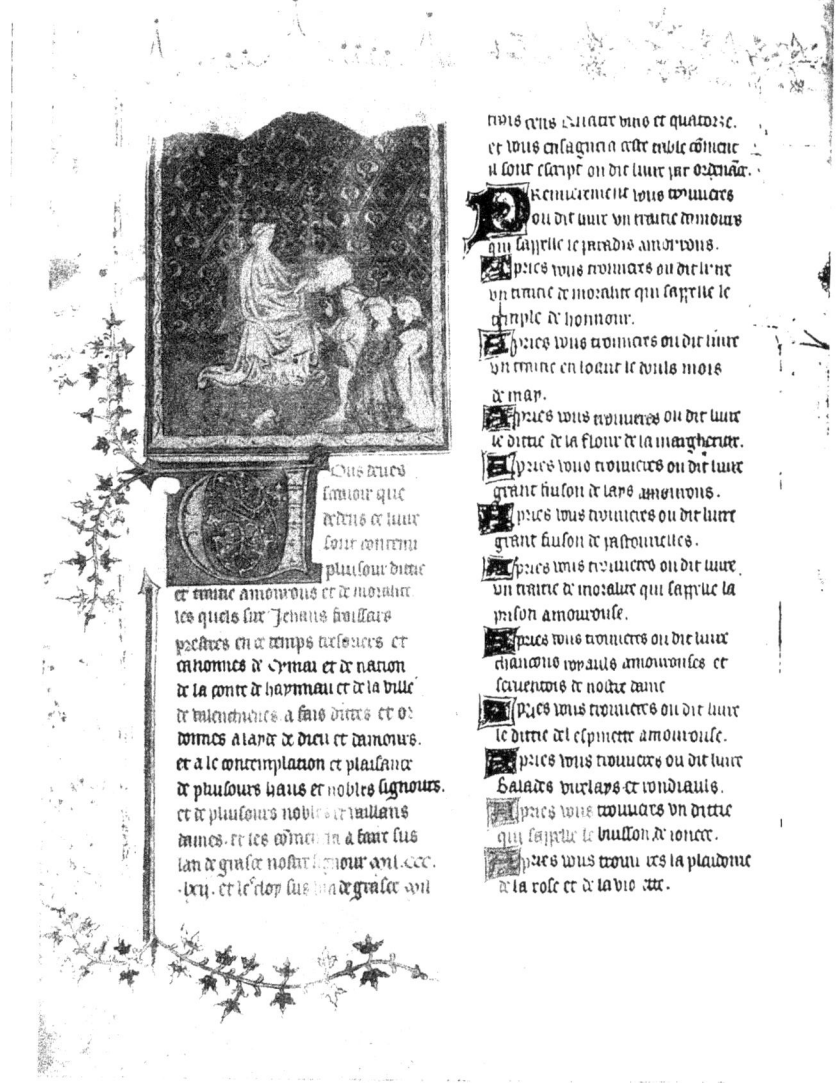

trois ans durant uins et quatorze.
et vous enfaigneia cefte table coment
il font efcript ou dit luir par ordenance.

Premierement vous trouuares
ou dit luir vn traitie damours
qui sappelle le paradis amoureus.

Apres vous trouuares ou dit liure
vn traitie de moralite qui sapelle le
temple d'honnour.

Apres vous trouuares ou dit liure
vn traitie en loeur de touls mois
de may.

Apres vous trouueres ou dit luir
le dittie de la flour de la margherite.

Apres vous trouueres ou dit liure
grant fuison de lays amoureus.

Apres vous trouuares ou dit liure
grant fuison de pastourelles.

Apres vous trouueres ou dit liure
vn traitie de moralite qui sapelle la
prison amoureuse.

Apres vous trouueres ou dit liure
chancons royauls amoureuses et
feruentois de nostre dame.

Apres vous trouueres ou dit liure
le dittie del espinette amoureuse.

Apres vous trouuares ou dit liure
balades virlays et rondiauls.

Apres vous trouuares vn dittie
qui sapelle le buisson de ionece.

Apres vous trouu[er]es la plaidoirie
de la rose et de la vio[lete].

Vous devés
sauoir que
dedens ce liure
sont contenu
plusour dittie
et traitie amoureus et de moralite
les quels fist Jehans froissars
prestres en ce temps tresoriers et
canonnes de Cymai et de nation
de la conte de haynnau et de la ville
de Valencennes a fais dittes et or-
donnes a lame de dieu et damours.
et a le contemplation et plaisance
de plusours haus et nobles signours.
et de plusours nobles et vaillans
dames. et les comencha a faire l'us
lan de grase nostre signour mil ccc.
lxxi. et le trop fut l'an de grase mil

FACSIMILE OF PAGE IN MS. OF FROISSART'S *DITTIERS AMOUREUS.* 1496.

Founding universities and endowing libraries were beyond the range of her expenditure, but she contributed her mite towards encouraging the zest for learning that was beginning to animate Europe to new intellectual activity. Various individuals eager to prosecute their studies were aided by her. Fifty gilders here, fifty gilders there, helped many a youth who longed to explore the mysteries of the philosophical researches at Cologne forbidden in the lesser schools. Her protégés did not, apparently, seek Louvain.

In the years that passed after the Treaty of Delft the exhausted little northern provinces seem to have slipped out of the stream of action into a back water, while various European complications floated by. The relations between England and Burgundy, whose maintenance had seriously affected Jacqueline's own fortunes, became more and more strained. The death of the Duchess of Bedford snapped an important link between the Burgundian family and the regent. When the latter married Jacquet of

254   A Mediæval Princess

Luxemburg out of hand, with scant courtesy to the memory of his wife, and without informing his late brother of Burgundy about his intentions until they became fact, an irreparable breach was made.

The apparent failure which overwhelmed the Maid of Orleans at Compiègne, the scene of little "Vrouw Jacob's" infant betrothal and early widowhood, Jeanne's sale by John of Luxemburg to the English, her imprisonment, her trial and tragic death in 1431,—all passed during the period when Jacqueline was living quietly in Zealand. The hands crushing the two valiant young women in their harness were the same. Philip of Burgundy, Cardinal Beaufort, once Bishop of Winchester, John of Bedford, all had a share, active or passive, in the burning of the one as they had in the discomfiture of the other

The result of Jeanne's sacrifice did not vanish in the smoke of her fagots. English domination was not sufficiently deep-rooted in France to withstand long the shock received at Orleans. The coronation of Henry VI at Paris did not efface the consecration of Charles VII at Rheims. When Philip at last addressed the latter as King of France and refused that title in his despatches to the former in a fashion to make the little sovereign weep, there was a seal set on English rule across the Channel.

At the death of the Duke of Bedford in 1435, it became clear how much his individuality had counted in giving prestige to his nephew's royalty.

With him "England lost all that had given great, noble, or statesmanlike elements to her attempts to hold France."[1] His successor as regent, the Duke of York, found the English dominion entrusted to him shrinking like a snow-ball before the rays of the sun of France. Soon the Treaty of Arras defined the new condition of affairs. Philip received and accepted apologies for his father's murder, was himself absolved by the cardinals from his oath of alliance with the English, and welcomed Charles VII

[1] Stubbs, *Constitutional History of England*, iii., p. 121.

into his own again. By the early summer
of 1436, the energetic duke was prepared
to besiege Calais and to dislodge his late
allies from that important foothold. Meanwhile, Humphrey, now last surviving son of
Henry IV, indignant at the Treaty of Arras,
which denied England the fruits of her long
wars, gathered a force and sailed over the
water with ten thousand men and two
hundred ships to defend his ward's choicest
continental possession. Calais, at least, was
saved to the English crown. The defender
then proceeded to carry war into Burgundian territories, and made a brief campaign on Flemish soil, where he wrought
much damage but failed to sustain his
own arrogant claim to wear the title of
"Count of Flanders," conferred upon him
by Henry VI as King of France, suzerain
of the land.[1] Philip, it was alleged, had
forfeited his rights by treachery to his liege
lord.

Of all Humphrey's uneasy pretensions
none were more absurd than this. His

[1] Holinshed, iii., p. 614.

expedition added nothing to his reputation or to his nephew's realm.

> "The protectour with his flete at Calys then,
> Did lande, and rode into Flaunders a little waye,
> And little did to counte a manly man,

writes a rhyming chronicler with no great admiration for the patron of letters.[1]

This abortive effort of the sometime Count of Holland, Zealand, and Hainaut by virtue of his marriage, to pose as count of another Netherland province might have been a source of amusement to Jacqueline. Lord Frank was deputed by his liege lord of Burgundy to be on the alert to repulse the English from the coast of Zealand. But there was no need. Humphrey's ships did not effect a landing. In alarm at the injury to commerce from the breach with Burgundy, the privy council addressed letters to some of the Holland cities and to Jacqueline herself, begging aid and co-operation. The draught of one signed by the young king, dated "March 29, 1436," is preserved with

[1] *The Chronicle of John Hardyng*, p. 396.

its erasures and changes.¹ It is addressed to *A ñre treschiere t tsamee* ~~marine~~ [*cousine t*] *mareine Jaque ducesse de Holande t Zeland tc.* ~~ñre tschre t~~ . . . . The affectionate "aunt" of the early communications has vanished, but other links are remembered. It is Jacqueline's turn to be reminded how her arm had held the infant prince at the font, and how she was still godmother to Henry VI, in spite of the mutations of circumstance. Her reply is not preserved. Certainly no aid was given to the English and the "Count of Flanders" discarded the term as he had his other Netherland designations. Perhaps, in later days, he wished he had shown courage in holding to the title of Count of Holland, once worn so flauntingly in the face of Europe, and to the cause of the woman from whom he received it, when "happened a miserable incident that served to show how powerless was Gloucester, or contemptibly pusillanimous."²

¹ *Proceedings,* etc., Nicolas, iv., p. 334.
² Stubbs, iii., p. 127. *Rot. Parl.,* v., p. 445.

In 1431, Eleanor Cobham, by that period fully acknowledged as Duke Humphrey's legal wife, was in her turn received into the fraternity at St. Albans as Jacqueline had been in 1423.[1] For a time she was first lady in the kingdom, but terribly evil days were in store for her. Ten years after this public reception by the good monks, this unhappy Duchess of Gloucester was convicted of treasonable witchcraft and condemned to life imprisonment, after doing humiliating penance by walking barefoot through London streets with a two-pound taper in her hand.[2] The crime charged against Eleanor Cobham was that she had tried to compass the death of Henry VI by fashioning a little waxen image in his likeness and melting it before a slow fire. Marjory Jordan suffered more severely for her aid in this plot, as she was convicted of witchcraft and burned at the stake.

[1] In this year the abbot appealed to Humphrey for aid in a quarrel with the Bishop. The courtesy to Eleanor may have been offered to gain her husband's friendly offices. *Annales Monasterii Sancti Albani*, Amundesham, p. 308. *Chronicon, ibid.*, p. 66.

[2] Stow, p. 381. Stubbs, iii., p. 127. See also Shakespeare, *Henry VI*, Part II, Act i., sc. ii.

When word came to Eleanor's ears that, from the pulpit at St. Paul's Cross on July 25th, St. James's Day, she had been publicly accused of being the principal in the witch's evil deed, she fled hastily to the shelter of Westminster. But the sanctuary did not avail to protect her from arrest, nor did her husband, although it is evident that the end of the plot was to pave his way to the throne. Afraid of being involved in her ruin, "he took all things patiently and said nothing."[1] Humphrey had learned patience under the affliction of others' misfortunes. Later, it is true, he made a futile effort to enact a law providing for the trial of noble ladies by their peers, and he was endeavouring to secure a definite pardon for Eleanor when he met his own unexplained death, out of favour with the royal nephew to whose interests he had ruthlessly sacrificed one woman. Whatever the decision of the Roman curia in regard to the invalidity of the Brabant marriage from the beginning, there was cer-

[1] *Grafton*, p. 588. See *Dict. Nat. Biog.*, vol. xxviii.

HUMPHREY, DUKE OF GLOUCESTER, AND ELEANOR HIS WIFE, RECEIVED
INTO THE CONFRATERNITY OF ST. ALBANS. 1431.

British Museum, MS. Col. Nero, D. VII.

tainly no adequate obstacle to a new marriage after John of Brabant's death [1] had left Jacqueline free to form an alliance where she would.

This humiliating calamity to her rival, which the sometime Duchess of Gloucester might have regarded as time's revenges for her own tragic desertion, did not occur until 1441, when all life's changes had ceased for Jacqueline.

[1] The statement that the Pope forbade any union between Jacqueline and Humphrey even if she were a widow seems unsustained by the terms of the bulls.

CHAPTER XV

Her Last Will

1436

A BRIEF space of two years was given to the "Countess of Ostrevant" to enjoy her last hazard of new fortunes, which assuredly secured tranquillity and freedom from anxiety to her and, possibly, more happiness than she had known since her father's death. If we may take phrases at their face value, Lord Frank was a much loved comrade. Every word of reference seems weighted with affection beyond the verbiage of legal courtesy.

In the summer of 1436, at about the time when Humphrey entered Flanders, Jacqueline was attacked by consumption. The disease developed rapidly and nothing availed to check its ravages, though Master

Her Last Will

John of Leyden and Master Gijsbrecht of Amsterdam were called in to aid Master Martin, her leech in ordinary, with their science. The two spent ninety-eight days at Teylingen, wrestling with the malady. Master Gillis, too, was summoned from Dordrecht to see if his greater skill could devise further remedies.

Like many consumptives, Jacqueline clung passionately to the earthly existence that had been none too sweet. During those weary days when she was evidently an acknowledged invalid, she was in no haste to arrange her affairs and make the last disposition of her worldly goods. She was young, having attained only her thirty-fifth year on July 25th, and it was natural that she should still cherish a hope that there were yet many years in store for her.

Three beguines or lay sisters and two holy brothers from Leiderdorp watched by her bedside to give her spiritual comfort. Thither, too, came Floris van Kyfhoek, Floris van Abele, and William van Egmont, councillors of the Court of Holland, besides her husband and her mother This last seems to have enjoyed an iron constitution. More than fifty years had elapsed since her marriage, but she was still apparently hale and hearty and ready to take responsibilities.

On Saturday, October 8th, the patient was warned that her case was beyond medical skill and that she must be prepared for the worst. Only then did she consent to make her will.[1] With her last breath she dictated her wishes to her faithful secretary, Jan Grenier. The Dowager, Lord Frank, and the three above-mentioned councillors were appointed as "testamentors" or executors to carry out her behests.

It was none too soon. Possibly the diseased lungs were strained by the effort of dictation. On the morrow, Sunday, October 9th, Jacqueline breathed her last.

Among those final desires was the expression of a wish to be carried to the chapel of the Borselen castle of St. Martensdijk— the castle where tradition says that her

[1] *Codex Diplomaticus Neerlandicus.* "Hist. Genoot. te Utrecht," 1852, pp. 166–266. The reckoning of the will is given in full.

heart was first touched by the delicate attention of the twisted *D's,* designed to express the Zealand noble's silent and humble devotion, and where the records show that she certainly gave him her hand in marriage. This natural wish was overruled by her executors, and "Dame Jaque" was buried among her ancestors at The Hague; not because that was the fitting sepulchre for the last child of the ancient House of Holland, but because forsooth the executors thought that the funeral would cost less![1] This fact appears in the final accounting of her will, filed away eight years after the deposed Countess was laid among her ancestors. November 6, 1444, is the date of the document signed by Gerard Potter, setting forth in the minutest detail the disposition of the estate.

The selection of the burial-place caused great disappointment to the dean and canons of the church at St. Martensdijk, as they felt that they were cheated out of probable offerings to the lady's shrine. In consideration

Codex Dip., p. 214.

of this loss, the executors gave them six hundred Philip's *scilde,* and my lord of Ostrevant added a gift out of his own pocket to ensure a daily mass to console and aid the soul of the departed, besides satisfying the chapter.

As the cortège wound along the road from Teylingen to The Hague, a distance of about twenty miles, largesse to the sum of ninety-five groots was thrown broadcast to the poor, while the priests, nuns, clerks, vergers, scholars, and other good and honest persons received in all £7 5s.

At The Hague, the final obsequies were performed with all honour and pomp in the presence of a goodly number of nobles, but the occasion was not graced by the presence of Philip or his family. The official chief mourner was the wife of the governor of Holland. During the usual period after the funeral she attended high mass daily in state. In recognition of this gracious participation in the ceremonies she received a rosary of pearls and jewels.

The bill for the actual interment, exclusive

Her Last Will

of candles, was £4 18s. 6d. All this last outlay was paid from the estate and all was recorded by Gerard Potter. Nothing great or small is forgotten. In addition to the masses celebrated at The Hague and at St. Martensdijk, many others were sung to the peace of the departed, and every solemn service was duly rewarded. An honourable bachelor in divinity of a preaching order, one Brother Heynric Smit, otherwise known as "My Friend" (*Mijn Vrunt*) received thirty shillings for his offices. Jan de Bruyn had the gift of a gown in addition to his fee, because he was such a shabby fellow Some of the items touch very humble folk, who did not dream that their fame would survive for five centuries. Bet Beth, who carried a message, a woman who placed the chairs and cushions, six poor people who held the torches, and one Spon Jannegen, ready to "help when he could and who is a pitiful fellow,"—all are duly recorded with their tiny receipts for their wages.

The learned doctors who watched the patient with their store of learning, only to read the sentence plain to less instructed eyes, reckoned their services at a gilder a day. Master Jan's fee came to one hundred gilders. As his servant deserved a present and a "little something" was added for the doctor, the total sum receipted for was £8 16s. 2d. Master Gijsbrecht received a like sum, while Master Gillis, "called [one wonders why] Jan van Apeltaren," signed a receipt for twelve Philip's crowns and something over. The faithful beguines had fifteen shillings, while every one else attached to the castle, or coming thither during the last illness to bring a fish or a message, remembered just how much labour or shoe leather or sabot wood it had cost them, and their claims were settled in full or in part.

The last service to the tomb was rendered by Joris, the sculptor, who carved a wooden figure in the late lady's image, to take its silent place among the effigies of the former counts and countesses of the land. His work was valued at two, his wood at five and a half *scilde*. Each *scild* being worth 2s. 4d., his whole bill was 17s. 6d. Joris's work has perished. We hear of it twenty-eight years after its making, when Dietrich van Duivenvoorde was obliged to pay thirty one ducats as a fine for his contemptuous words about it; and again at the end of the sixteenth century, when the States General decided that it needed a fresh coat of paint. Jacqueline's name lingered longer than that amid the branches of a tree she is said to have planted at Goes, and in a little copse in The Hague woods known as "Jacoba's Preeltje."[1]

The first steps toward settling the estate were taken promptly, even before the testator was laid away to rest. On October 12th, Lord Frank made a formal renunciation, present and future, of his wife's personal estate, and of all possible claims to sovereignty, and he was released from any responsibility for her debts. The Dowager Countess received the same release. Lord Frank retained the title of Count of Ostrevant with the accompanying income of five

[1] *Haagsche Jaarboekje,* 1892. It has been shown, however, that the *Jacob* of this name was a pastor, not the Countess.

hundred crowns.[1] Evidently the title was henceforth shorn of all suggestion that its bearer was the heir, either apparent or presumptive, to the sovereignty of the countships. During the thirty-five years that Lord Frank survived his wife, he was, as Count of Ostrevant, a prominent figure in the Burgundian court, addressed by the Duke as "cousin," and finally admitted among the elect in the Order of the Golden Fleece. Whether from devotion to Jacqueline's memory or from reluctance to sever his connection with her name, he remained a widower.[2]

The reason for Borselen's renunciation of Jacqueline's personal estate is plain. It was barely sufficient to cover her bequests and the task of her executors was no sinecure. Countess Margaret asked and obtained permission to have Jan van der Mije act as her attorney, because she could not be present continually, while Lord Frank appointed Jan

---

[1] Coinage of Philip of Burgundy. Certain estates not touched by his oath also fell to him as provided in the marriage settlements.

[2] He died 1471. Reckoning of his estate, *Codex Dip.*, 1852, p. 147.

THE STATUE OF JEANNE D'ARC AT COMPIÈGNE.

Ruyschrock "to help in his name as best he could."

The testament was confirmed without delay by Philip, who chanced to be at Damme. His letters patent, declaring that the last wishes of his late rival should be fulfilled, are dated October 11th, and a copy was filed with the will. There were thus no protests to encounter, no law's delays, yet eight years elapsed before the business of settlement was completed and the account filed away in The Hague archives, where it has rested, over four and a half centuries.

The first act of the executors was to realise the cash value of the testator's possessions in order to give peace to her soul by doing God's will and by satisfying her poor servants.[2] The inventory of the personal property is almost pitiful in its minuteness, laying bare every recess of Jacqueline's household. Significant of the loose and uncertain state of the currency is the list of

---
[1] *Codex Dip.*, p. 167.
[2] *Om dair off ter ʒ yelen troest om Gods wille te geven, hair arme dienres mede te lonen.*

coins receivable in the sale. To the long enumeration is added the phrase, "and all other gold and silver at such price as the following reckoning stipulates."[1]

The jewels were the first articles sold. From Bruges, Dordrecht, and other places merchants flocked to The Hague. Among them was one, Jan Puyctinck, commonly known as "Uncle Goldcup,"—*Goidscale Oom*.[2] Thus he is designated when he purchased one lot of gems, chains, and other valuables. At another time, "Uncle Goldcup" is mentioned as buying "in behalf of Jan Puyctinck." Perhaps the recording clerk was confused with "Uncle Goldcup's" numerous purchases, for he invested largely. Beatrice Colyns, one of the household and herself a legatee, buys in, among other things, a white flower studded with two pearls and a diamond. She also bought one ring out of a lot of three, which all together were not worth more than six shillings. When it was discovered how

Codex, p. 167.
[2] *Goidscale Oom eenen coopman van Brugge geheten Ja Puyctinck.*

trifling in value was her purchase, the other two rings were given her to boot.

Two sable sleeves, almost as treasured as the jewels, were bought by Jehan de Bull for £14. Angel sleeves they must have been, and very large at that, if the statement that they contained 296 sables be not a clerical error or a later misprint.[1]

Among the jewel cases, preserved as carefully as precious stones themselves, were six English books. Some were on history and some on medicine, but as they were written in English, "here in the land there was no one to reap profit" from their contents, and they were sold to an unknown English merchant for £5 16s. 8d.

The total amount received for these valuables, excluding those specifically bequeathed, was £1382 7s. 8½d., and the approximate value of this sum may be estimated by the price paid for seventeen horses and ten cows in the stable—£59 12s. 4d.

[1] It was the age of "sleeves that slod upon the earth" quotes Trevelyan in the *Age of Wycliffe* (p. 63), and the fashion continued into the fifteenth century.

The sale of all the household effects followed that of the special treasures. The very beds from the various dwellings were not spared: twelve from St. Martensdijk, sixteen from Hoochstraten, thirty-two from Oostvoorn, with all their appurtenances, were carried off to humbler homes. The kitchen utensils, great and small, were turned over to Jan van der Mije, and those of any value were sold at Dordrecht "to the profit of my lord of Ostrevant." A few pots and pans were excepted and given outright to the women present at the masses celebrated on the octave and the thirtieth day after Jacqueline's death. Everything left in the larder after the funeral baked meats had been served, even the very salt, beer, and vinegar, were also disposed of in the market at Dordrecht, for £6 9s. For all the little articles left in the various houses unaccounted for specifically, Lord Frank paid the estate a lump sum of one hundred Philip's *scilde*.

Some of the clothes were reserved from the sale and bestowed on ladies or maids of the household. It is pleasant to read that a poor "wifekin" became the recipient of a little cloak, even though the same were not lined.[1] One lot containing an old coat, a hood, two or three rosaries and some other articles of no value were distributed to various people, "whose names are forgotten," records Gerard Potter's clerk. Other garments were presented to cloisters in acknowledgment whereof masses were sung, while Jan the barber picked out a certain black silk tabbert as promised him by his late mistress, and his unattested word was believed. To Ermgart van Rietuelt and Juffrouw Hastgen, faithful watchers at the sick-bed of their lady, was given a chest of miscellaneous contents. Ermgart was to receive two-thirds for her longer service and Hastgen the remainder. Honest to the end the women proved themselves. Among the other things rightfully theirs, they discovered some pearls, which they recognised as the property of their

[1] *Een zwart cleyn eenwissel huyckin om Gods gegeven een arm wijffken.*

late lady's mother, and straightway they surrendered the jewels to the Dowager.

When all the personal property was realised, the settlement of the bequests began. The desire to "satisfy her poor servants" was evidently strong in those last hours of the dying lady, so many did she try to provide for by name. Then, too, she seems to have longed to compensate for certain wrongs committed in her time if not in her name. Four hundred masses were provided for the soul of one Gillis, cook to her late uncle, John of Bavaria. This man had met a violent death in England, and there were rumours that he had had some hand in the plots against John's life. The kinsman implicated in the murder of Willem van der Berg, the Brabantine treasurer, received a special bequest to pay the fine still due to the murderer's family. During his wife's lifetime Lord Frank had pledged himself to see that this sum was paid, but evidently the pledge was still unfulfilled in 1436. That Jacqueline showed an interest in the criminal must not however be taken as a proof

Her Last Will

of her co-operation in the crime, as has been urged. Abundant evidence exists of her kindly interest in many of her connections whether she knew them or not. "A certain Vrouw Kerstine claiming to be my lady's sister dwelling with her daughter at Utrecht," was bequeathed a black gown and one hundred and fifty *scilde* to buy her daughter's admission into a close sisterhood at The Hague.

Churches, cloisters, and other religious foundations throughout the three lands received many presents, sometimes for their poor, sometimes to ensure prayers for "Dame Jaque" All who took part in the celebration of the masses at the stipulated anniversaries had a recompense of some kind.

The executors were further besieged by a shower of miscellaneous claims against the estate. There were excellent memories on the part of all who had ever rendered any service to Jacqueline. "A certain great prior" said that he had furnished the coin for largesse on one occasion, and many old servants, chiefly cooks, declared that they had lent their mistress money at various times. In several instances the claim was not allowed as valid, but something was given because of the poverty of the claimant. Occasionally the claim is endorsed *néant payé*. Sometimes there is a plea that the petitioner suffered loss in the lady's service from the death of a horse. Another, perhaps, had worn out time and shoes in journeying on foot to a shrine to pray for the success of his lady's struggle to regain her sovereignty. Again there were requests frankly for the benefit of the petitioner who had cherished some kindly word spoken by Jacqueline and thought it a promise.

One of her student beneficiaries at Cologne asserted that his patroness had further promised him means to give a supper when he was *doctoryzed*. Fifty Rhenish gilders were allowed to celebrate his academic success, so that a grand banquet should be given and a stately feast be held.[1] His quittance shows an acknowledgment for £8 2s. 7d.

[1] *Eene groote maeltyt geven ende een statelyke feeste houden soude.*

Not alone were the testator's own debts and obligations, formal and informal, considered, but ancient claims against her father were brought to light. One Bartelmeus van Bleeswijc presented a bill for broideries wrought at Count William's order at the time of "Dame Jaque's marriage to Duke John of Touraine."[1] "Our lady had, to be sure, repudiated all such indebtedness but, admitting that Bleeswijc had more right than the other creditors, she had given him, as an especial favour, an order for one hundred francs," each piece valued at 16s. Parisian. This order had never been fulfilled. It was finally honoured, but paid in coins worth less than the value stipulated.

Coincident with the demands of the claimants were the efforts of the lawyers to collect all outstanding moneys owed to the testator. As late as 1440, Philip sent heralds through the lands to search out his predecessor's debtors. Dirc Lieue spent a fortnight in South Beveland on this quest. Sixteen shillings were charged to the estate for his

[1] *Codex*, p. 244.

expenses, because it was hard travelling in December. These Zealanders had been dunned several times for back taxes. Now they were warned that their mills would be stopped until they paid or the Duke would collect by force.

When all claims were settled in full or compounded at the amount the estate could afford, then came the accounts of the legal expenses incidental to the business. Here, too, we find evidences of good memories. Jan Grenier received thirty shillings for drawing up the instrument, and Joriken, his servant, came in for four shillings, as he had helped in the task, besides writing the letter of notification to the Duke of Burgundy. The lists of jewels, etc., made first in Latin and then translated into the vernacular were an extra item of expense Then there were the Delft goldsmiths who came to The Hague to appraise the jewels, and the legal experts summoned to test the validity of the will. The latter discussed affairs over a dinner in company with some of the executors at the "Ooltgens." This cost the estate twelve shillings, and similar refections on other occasions were duly accounted for, showing an admixture of business and pleasure. When Floris van Abele, Floris van Kyfhoek, and Jan van der Mije journeyed to Brill in "the week before mid-Lent" to have their papers inspected by their liege lord, their wagon and boat hire amounted to thirteen shillings and eight pence. Trips to Brussels, to Haarlem, and elsewhere, where the Duke of Burgundy might chance to be in the course of his peripatetic administration, were more or less costly, according to the rank of the messenger. The outlay on ink, parchment, and paper during the eight years is lumped at £2.

At last every item was settled and Gerard Potter filed away his papers in the archives, unconscious chroniclers of Jacqueline and of her surroundings. The items touched on here are only a few of many, all eloquent with suggestions as to how life actually passed in the household of a fifteenth-century Holland dame.

CHAPTER XVI

The Lady and the Land

FACT and fiction, rhyme and charter reason, admiration and calumny are closely interwoven into the woof of Jacqueline's story as it may be gathered piecemeal from witnesses of her own time, or as it is rewritten by authors in the succeeding centuries. She is a romantic heroine, the embodiment of a national feeling, the personification of mediævalism with a nimbus of chivalry, a charming, spirited creature, courageous under adverse circumstances, battling sturdily for her rights against arrant injustice. Again, she is an undisciplined, lawless person,[1] whose hereditary claims were properly set aside because she was unequal to the task bequeathed to her by her

---

[1] Her most merciless critic is Bilderdijk, whose animosity is carried to an amusing pitch. See *Dichtwerken,* i., p. 216; xiv., p. 17.

father, and because she defied the laws of the Church and of society. What she wanted, fragments of what she did and said are easy to know. The tales of documents, proclamations, and municipal records, of privy council discussions and contemporaneous chronicles, lie open to the reader. But what manner of woman she really was, even whether she were beautiful or not, or what was her outward semblance at the earlier phase of her career, are questions difficult to solve. The fact of her public betrothal makes the little maiden a definite historic personage at the age of four and the barren details suggest dimly a bewitching baby form, decked out in pompous bravery of ceremonial array. No portraits remain of her as Daughter, as Duchess of Touraine, or as Dauphiness, although the presence of one Guisquin Zalm,[1] artist, in the suite of the French bridegroom permits the inference that the *promessi sposi* were depicted in some fashion, but the result has vanished as well as all work from the hands of any

[1] Or Salm—*Cartulaire,* iv., p. v.

painter employed by Jacqueline's father, but undoubtedly some portraits once existed.

Count William's miniature court, migratory between Holland and Hainaut, had all the features of larger princely households. No uncouth feudal overlord was this last petty sovereign in Hainaut. He shines out as a brilliant figure on the delightful pages of that vivacious chronicler, Froissart, his own fellow-countryman. There he is, alert for any adventure, a typical scion of the spirit of knighthood as it flowers in mediæval literature of an earlier period. His travels made him a man of the world, at home in many places besides the province imbedded in forests and feudalism, or in his native Holland, then at the dawn of her commercial enterprise. The very day when, as Count of Ostrevant, William VI won his spurs, "he reared up his baner and quytte himselfe lyke a good knight." Later at a famous tourney in London,[1] "Syr Gyllyam of Heynalt, erle of Ostrevant, justed ryght

[1] *The Cronycle of Syr John Froissart,* Tudor Translation, iv., p. 39; v., p. 285. The quaint English seems to interpret the author better than later versions.

MS. VOLUME OF FROISSART.
Containing comments on Jacqueline.

goodly—and so dyd such knyghtes as came with him ; all dyde well their devoyre to the prays of the ladys." The sojourn in London was delightful and left such agreeable memories that William was eager to repeat the experience in 1390, when the voice of an English herald resounded through the Netherlands, bidding all good knights hasten over the sea to take part in the gaieties celebrating the entry of King Richard's young bride, Isabel, into London.[1] To his father's remonstrance that he did not wish his "fayre son" to be involved in English affairs, William replies, "Dere father, I wyll nat go into Englande to make any alyaunce ; I do it but to feest and make myrthe with my cousins there and because the feest whiche shal be holden at London is publisshed abrode ; wherefore syth I am signifyed therof and shulde nat go thyder it shulde be sayd I were proude and presumptuous." "Sonne, do as ye lyste ; but I thynke surely it wére better that ye taryed at home," was Count Albert's last word,

[1] *The Cronycle of Syr John Froissart*, vi., p. 420.

which the son interpreted as permission in lieu of more hearty approval of his plan. "On a Thursday he passed over and so came to Canterbury and on the Fridaye he visited saint Thomas shrine and because he had so gret a company and cariages, he rode but small journeys to ease his horse and on the Sondaye he rode to dyner to Dertforde and after dyner to London to be at the feast which began the same Sonday "

Gay indeed the occasion proved and great was the renown attained by the gallant visitor from Holland. He hesitated a little as to the wisdom of accepting the final honour conferred on him,—the Garter, but finally he is admitted into that order, to the annoyance of the French courtiers, who murmur, " The erle of Ostrevaunt sheweth well that his courage enclyneth rather to be Eng lysshe than Frenche when he taketh on hym the order of the garter and weareth the kynge of Englandes device. . . . . The tyme wyll come he shall repent hym selfe." They thought it especially ill-judged because the Count of Ostrevant had always been more highly favoured in Paris than any other of the French king's cousins. Froissart thinks that these gentlemen were unduly critical of William. "For that he dyde was but for love and good company; howbeit no man canne let the envyous to speke yvell."

The historian proceeds to relate how these same nobles, on their return to Paris, made capital out of this event and tried to bring discredit on the Netherland count by reiterating that he was "become the kynge of Englande's man."

This was a title certainly not acknowledged by Count William, but friends with England he was and remained. Froissart himself consults him in regard to his own projected visit to Richard II. in 1395, because his experience was of later date than the historian's. From time to time, travellers arrive in Hainaut and remind the Count of former acquaintance in London. Thither comes the banished Henry of Lancaster on that journey of exile whence he

returns home to take the crown from h[is]
royal cousin, and to Jacqueline Henry
requited the hospitality once offered by h[is]
father to his own.

In his love for adventure William go[es]
east as well as west. He saw Prussia a[nd]
longed to participate in an expedition [to]
Hungary and thence to Turkey. Wh[en]
he begs his father's sanction to this la[st]
scheme, Count Albert, "as a man redy p[ur]veyed of aunswere sayd 'Guylliam wh[at]
haste or wyll have you to go this voya[ge]
into Hungery and into Turkey to seke arm[es]
upon people and countrey that never dyd
any forfeyte? Thou hast no tytell of reas[on]
to go but for the vayne glory of the worlc[le]
. Go thou into Frese and conque[r]
our herytage that these Fresones by pri[de]
and rudenes do witholde from us.'" Tl[his]
suggestion was not unpleasing to the "hei[r]
of therle of Ostrevant." "My lorde ye sa[y]
well and if it please you that I shall do tl[his]
voyage I shall do it with ryght a go[od]
wyll," was the son's dutiful reply.

To Friesland, accordingly, the young w[ar]

rior turned his attention. His campaign in that territory was so far successful that he recovered and brought back to Holland the bones of his grand-uncle, who had found an untimely and unhonoured grave in his own Friesland enterprise. The remains of William IV were, however, all that the Frisians really lost. In the following year they made good everything else, and William VI never again found time to enforce the assertion of Holland's supremacy in that region, having his hands full with incessant party quarrels at home.

The abrupt manner in which Count William rushed away from London in 1416, his departure from Paris in 1417, are incidents showing that the middle-aged man did not change essentially as years went by from the impulsive youth, agog at the suggestion of a new quest and prone to let speedy action follow a sudden thought. Margaret of Burgundy was not a particularly congenial consort to her husband. She was more subtle in her nature than he. She was addicted to political intrigue, and she was animated in her plotting by Burgundian ambition and craft, though she was certainly less skilful in attaining her ends than other members of her family. Count William amused himself with other women more to his taste than the partner of a political alliance, but rumour says that he was a devoted father to his daughter. Certainly during the later years of his life he was deeply preoccupied with plans for Jacqueline's future.

When not abroad or afield on his various quests of business, of pleasure, and of war, Count William's life at The Hague, at Bouchain, or Quesnoy was filled with strenuous amusement and with gay pastime. His lion-pit was renowned far and wide, so, too, were his harpers, his falcons, his blooded steeds his minstrels. Two, at least, of the poets once haunting his court are known to posterity, Dirc Potter and William van Hildegaersberch. The former, author of *Der Minnen Loep,* "The Course of Love," is moreover, mentioned as *mijn liefs herer clerc,* "my dear lord's clerk," and received many a gilder for his diplomatic services in addition to his verses. In later years Potter turned to bask in the favour of Burgundy, after reaping what harvest he could under John of Bavaria. "He preaches and he sings in order to have money jingle in his purse" is the characterisation of a bard as given by William van Hildegaersberch. Patronage was eagerly sought by the poetic aspirants to literary fame, and, as a rule, their aim was to please the higher classes.[1] Potter declares that the bourgeois world could not understand love, the theme of his pen. Yet both he and Hildegaersberch wrote in the vernacular and the virtues they lauded were those belonging to the middle class rather than to the aristocratic world

In Hainaut the charming and cultivated Froissart hardly crossed the threshold of the fifteenth century, and there was no successor in his art worthy to be classed on his level. Hildegaersberch spoke only his own tongue and depended for his subject

[1] *Nederlandsche Letterkunde*, W. J. A. Jonckbloet, ii., p. 242.

matter upon clerks, who translated for his benefit "many a theme writ in Latin." This William van Hildegaersberch is mentioned twenty times in the accounts of Hol land between 1383 and 1408. His works are devoted to moralisings, to abstruse speculations, and to allegories. There is little trace of divine fire in his lines. Only here and there occur quickened bits of narrative and well-turned dialogues. Much more is ascribed to him, however, than ever came from his pen, industrious as it was.

The accounts of Holland show that in addition to recitations and songs, dramatic representations were given at Count William's expense to amuse the courtiers. Both mysteries and moralities were acted, sometimes by "clericals" and again by "clericals and others." It is more than probable that *Everyman* was performed on The Hague stage, although actual record of such event is not forthcoming.

Such was the atmosphere in which Jacqueline grew to maturity,—romantic, full of amusement and of movement, essentially mediæval in tone, in colour, and in thought. Both virtues and failings leaned towards those of earlier centuries.

Exactly what system of education Count William arranged for his ward and his daughter in addition to instruction in the mysteries of falconry and the chase, it is difficult to state. Jacqueline spoke French, Dutch, perhaps some faulty Latin, and English. That this last language was little understood in spite of the marked similarity then existing between the speech heard in England and in the Netherlands, is proven by the chance phrase in Gerard Potter's statement that "none here in the land" could make any use of the six English books carefully preserved among Jacqueline's jewels.

Such history as was taught was mainly genealogical; lessons were given in heraldry, and possibly in some principles of the statecraft then in vogue, and in the feudal institutions as prevailing in city and country, though Löher's suggestion that there was definite training to prepare the future executives for their prospectives duties[1] is a trifle imaginative. Jacqueline was undoubtedly initiated into the use of the needle, though there is no indication that embroidery ever became an agreeable solace to her in weary hours. Then, too, she was tutored in the code of etiquette, with its rigid rules for the observance of outward forms, but no theory of conduct restrained her from unauthorised, unconventional action any more than it did her knightly father.

In the early decades of the fifteenth century education was just beginning to be a matter of concern to the lay world. Criticisms of abuses within the one dominant learned body, the Church, were current in the Netherlands even among those quite faithful to its tenets and without sympathy for the Lollards. The accusation that popes and priests wrought ill and were "deaf in their understanding," and "cared for naught but to count the florins," creeps out in the verses of Hildegaersberch and of other moralising rhymsters. But there was also a spirit

[1] Löher, i., p. 239.

of real faith active in the land, finding expression in establishments like that founded by Gerard de Groot at Deventer in 1385, where opportunities were furnished for the prosecution of other than theological studies.[1] This institution took quick root, prospered, and found imitators. By 1430, there were forty-five similar schools in Holland, frequented by adult scholars before any universities proper existed in the Netherlands.

As to lower education, some idea of methods may be obtained from the records of Leyden There the appointment of the schoolmaster was among the privileges sold outright by the Count of Holland to the burgrave. In 1351, that officer, then Dirk van Wassenaar, in his turn ceded the right of nomination to the city fathers, who hastened to buy a piece of land from Count Albert's own estate on which to erect a public schoolhouse.[2] Thenceforward the duty of selecting an instructor for the Leyden

---

[1] Blok, *Eene Holl. Stad in de Middeleeuwen*, p. 283.
[2] *Ibid.*, p. 297.

youth was vested in the town council, some supervision being exercised by the chapter of St. Peter's; but the incumbent of the office was released from fulfilling the duties of sexton as well as those of pedagogue, and municipal education thenceforth became a definite institution.

Just at the end of the fourteenth century a certain Jan of Hokelen, rector of St. Geertruidenberg, was appointed schoolmaster at Leyden for a term of four years. In his contract it is stipulated that he might carry on his own studies during the second half of his engagement, provided that he does so within thirty miles of Leyden, and that he procures a satisfactory substitute to perform his duties. He is especially enjoined to pay great attention to grammar and to logic in his course of instruction.

In 1408, we find that Jan of Haarlem, the then incumbent, was permitted to have as assistants two clerks, who also shared in the receipts. Jan's salary, irrespective of his portion of the fees, was £18 a year and a dwelling. Moreover, he was carefully protected against the vengeance of parents who might be disposed to resent the disciplining of their unruly offspring. Evidently this was no unlikely contingency. Friction between pupils and masters was occasionally so serious that the intervention of a higher power became necessary, and the worthy pedagogues were not invariably sustained in their authority. The fee due from the scholars, girls and boys alike, was sixteen shillings a year, but lads happily endowed with good voices were able to contribute something towards their own education. If they sang in the choir a small sum was deducted from their tuition bills.

In addition to this public academy, private schools, too, found patronage in Leyden. The accounts rendered by a certain guardian show the course pursued by three girls (1397-1406). Their education was begun at a private school, where the terms ran from May to All Saints' Day at a fee of ten shillings a term. From this establishment they passed on to the city school for half a year at eight shillings, and they were "finished" by taking sewing lessons from the beguines, for which a summer sufficed.

In the city school the pupils were drilled in Latin grammar until they were perfect in the *congruum* and *incongruum*. In logic they were to use a particular book as far as the *supposita* and *consequentia,* hypothesis and conclusion. Instruction in philosophy was expressly forbidden lest the children's minds should be confused.

The masters were not free to grant holidays as they would. Vacations lay wholly within municipal jurisdiction, but the pedagogues were protected from officious interference in their educational methods by the provision that no city messenger should have access to the school unless he carried a permit of visitation, duly signed by two burgomasters.

Paternal oversight was thus exercised by the town officials to guard the early training of the young and civic supervision of ideas did not cease with the children. The burgomasters not only restricted the school curriculum; they endeavoured to curb independence of thought about religious matters on the part of adult citizens. Cases of heresy came before the councils both at Leyden and at Mons during the early decades of the fifteenth century. Even then the authority of the Church was not unassailed. By 1417, copies of the Scriptures in the vernacular were read by zealous Lollards, who were under the ban, though less actively prosecuted than their brethren in England at the same period and a little later, by Humphrey of Gloucester, who was very vigorous in his determination to uproot the obnoxious sect.

But in all probability no harassing thought of doctrinal perplexity and little inspiration of new learning penetrated into Count William's court, or in any wise affected either him or his heiress. Jacqueline was a devout daughter of the Church and remained so in spite of her discontent with papal action in regard to her own much desired divorce. One of her earliest sovereign acts was the founding of the chapel at Bouchain, while many of her last testamentary provisions show interest in religious establishments of various kinds Brunelleschi had no contemporary in the Netherlands of equal skill, but there were efforts at ecclesiastical architecture at this epoch when the Florentine was erecting his dome, and in these efforts the young Countess assisted to the honour of the Church. Philosophy was as much unknown to her as to the Leyden school-children to whom its speculations were sealed by order of the burgomasters. Her mind looked without, not within. She was absorbed in the complications that beset her, not in the intricacies of intellectual life. Like her father, she was essentially a child of Hainaut in spite of the fact that she breathed her first breath and her last in the air of Holland.

Most of the descriptions of Jacqueline by her contemporaries show her in the open—on the battlefield,—standing upon the embankment at Calais straining her eyes to catch a glimpse of the white cliffs of England looming out of the March mist,—riding up to London from Dover, seated in dignified stateliness upon the palfrey, with Gloucester as her escort,—entering the courtyard of St. Albans, accompanied by twenty-four horse, on her road to Langley, —galloping away from Ghent in page's dress to meet the September dawn,—and finally making a slow and stately progress by the side of her conquering cousin through Holland, with gala array covering a sad heart, forced to proclaim to her subjects, both faithful and rebellious, her acquiescence in Philip's victory, her definite resignation in her own sorry defeat.

The painting which is said to represent Jacqueline at about the age of twenty depicts, however, a far more sedate personage than is suggested by any of the phrases sketching the above incidents in her career.

This picture is preserved in the museum at Copenhagen. It is the work of some unknown artist, said to be taken from an original by Jan van Eyck, which has disappeared but critics find sufficient evidences of the Flemish master's style in this copy on wood to be willing to accept the accuracy of the statement of its genesis.[1] If it be true, the question as to the date of execution becomes an interesting one. Van Eyck's biographers assume that this must have been during the period when the artist was in the services of John of Bavaria. The accounts of Henry Nothaft, treasurer of Holland, and his successor, fix this date exactly, the time when the painter and his assistants were busied upon the decorations of The Hague chapel, work that has also vanished. The first receipt for the wages of nine weeks and three days shows that the labour was commenced on October 24, 1422. Later entries indicate that Van Eyck ceased working for John about three months before the latter's death. During the entire period of his established sojourn in Holland, Jacqueline was not only on terms with her uncle which would have precluded her employing his protégé, but she was across the Channel in England, far out of reach of the painter's brush. Accordingly, the inference

[1] The copy is assignable to the end of the sixteenth century. See *Early Flemish Painters,* Crowe and Cavalcaselle, pp. 40, 42, and *Jan van Eyck,* L. Kaemmerer, 1902, p. 47.

that her portrait was contemporaneous with the lost frescoes at The Hague is manifestly absurd. Another theory that Van Eyck was in Antwerp in 1420, when he might have executed the work, has been abandoned by his latest biographer on what seem to be adequate grounds.

Granting the authenticity of Van Eyck's handiwork, another possibility as to its date may be considered. After May, 1425, the artist was in the employ of Philip of Burgundy.[1] The features of the portrait are certainly those of an older woman than Jacqueline was before her flight to England. Moreover, the head-dress worn is Burgundian in style May it not therefore be inferred that Van Eyck was commissioned by the Duke of Burgundy to execute the portrait of his defeated cousin as a fitting termination to the feasts of reconciliation? Such an action would have been eminently consistent with the character of Philip, delighted to make a display of his magnanimity.

[1] Payments were made to *Jehan de Heick jadiz pointre et varlet de Chambre de feu. M. S. le duc Jehan de Bayvière*, quoted, Crowe and Cavalcaselle, p. 42.

Shortly after the Treaty of Delft, Jan van Eyck went to Portugal with the embassy despatched to escort Philip's third bride to the Netherlands. Jacqueline might have sat for him in September, 1428. If not then, the date may be placed anywhere from 1430 to 1433. In such case she would have been about thirty, an age that tallies fairly well with the features of the Copenhagen copy.

Whether the portrait belongs to 1420, 1428, or 1431, it is interesting as being a reproduction of a contemporaneous study of Jacqueline's face. Here she certainly is not as beautiful as might be expected from descriptions.[1] Chastellain, himself three years her junior, calls her young, gay, and vigorous. Monstrelet says she was in the flower of her age beautiful, well formed, and endowed with an excellent understanding, words used again by Vinchant and other later chroniclers. Various other authors ascribe beauty to her, perhaps only because it seems the natural attribute of a youthful

---

[1] Chastellain, i., chap. 71; Monstrelet, iv., i., chap. 236, p. 27; Vinchant, iv., p. 71.

princess. One curious bit of casual testimony, plain as when it came from the hand of a contemporary, however, gives a less flattering comment upon her looks.

In the National Library at Paris there rests a little manuscript volume[1] entitled *" Dittiers et traittiers amoureus—par discret et vénérable homme sire Jehan Froissart."* On the fly leaves of the book, various phrases have been written by different hands. Some are fairly legible:

"Ce livre est a Richart le gentil feals conte de Warrewyck."

"C'est bien raison dit Jaque de Baviere."

" R. Raison pour guy pour ce que je veiss as freres."

"Plus leide ny a Jacque de Baviere. Plus belle ny a que my [ma mie ?] Warigny."

On another leaf, among other lines occur the following:

"Beau promettre et rien doner fait la fole recomforter dit Dorvic."

"Sans plus la laide Jaque dit Gloucestre

"La meins amee est Jaque"

[1] No. 831. *Œuvres de Froissart,* ed. Aug. Scheler, Bruxelles, 1870, i., p. xv.

"Nulle si belle dit Warigny."
"Cest bien raison dit Jacque
Sans plus vous belle Gloucestre."

At the bottom of this page is a heart composed of two hearts. This last seems to be of a later date.

Froissart has left his own statement in regard to the contents of this little collection of his verses.[1] When he mentions his desire to revisit England in 1395, he adds: "And I had engrosed in a fayre boke well enlumyned, all the matters of amours and moralytees that in four and twentie yeres before I hadde made and compyled, whiche greatly quickened my desyre to go into Englande to se king Rycharde. . . . . Also I hadde this said fayre boke well covered with velvet garnysshed with clapses of sylver and gylte, therof to make a present to the kynge at my fyrst commynge to his presence."

The project was carried out, and Froissart crossed the sea armed with letters from

[1] *Froissart*, vi., pp. 130, 147.

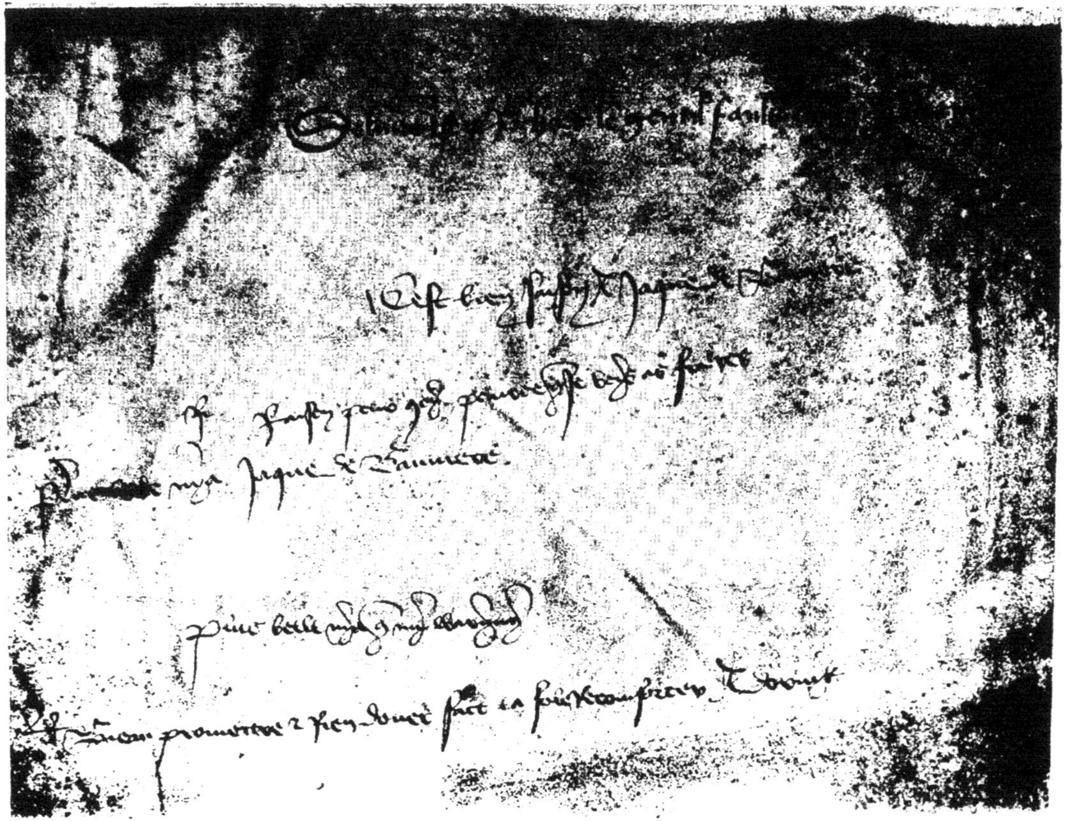

Counts Albert and William to recommend him to King Richard, whom the poet had only seen on the day when he was carried to the font. The court was at Leeds. Thither the traveller journeyed, was admitted to the royal presence, and delivered up his letters, but Richard was so busy that "on that day I shewed not the kynge the boke that I hadde brought for hym"

Many days elapsed before the moment seemed ripe for presentation of the cherished gift. It was at Eltham that "lorde Thomas Percy and syr Rycharde Sury shewed my busynesse to the kynge. Then the kynge desired to se my book that I had brought for hym; so he sawe it in his chambre, for I had layde it there redy on his bedde. Whanne the kynge opened it, it pleased hym well for it was fayre enlumined and written, and covered with crymson velvet with ten botons of sylver and gylte, and roses of gold in the myddes, with two great claspses gylte, rychely wrought. Then the kyng demaunded me whereof it treated, and I shewed hym how it treated of maters of love; wherof the kynge was gladde and loked in it and reed it in many places, for he coulde speke and rede Frenche very well; and he tooke it to a knyght of hys chambre named syr Richarde Creadon to beare it into his secret chambre."

The cover of the volume at Paris is not velvet, nor is it garnished with clasps of silver and gilt. The date when it was written, 1394, corresponds, however, with that given by Froissart. It may be that a replica of the presentation volume was made for the then Earl of Warwick and bound less sumptuously. By 1426, the elder earl was dead and his son, Richard, was in Paris, as appears from a few lines by Lydgate, written when

"Henry the sext of Age ny fyve yere reni
  I moved was   . by . . commande-
    ment
  Of . . . my lord of Warrewyk
  Being present that tyme at parys."[1]

This year 1426, when Richard de Beau-

---

[1] Lydgate's *Temple of Glas*. Ed. J. Schick. See Introduction, p. xciii. Meaning of *reni* is unknown. Can it be "reigned"?

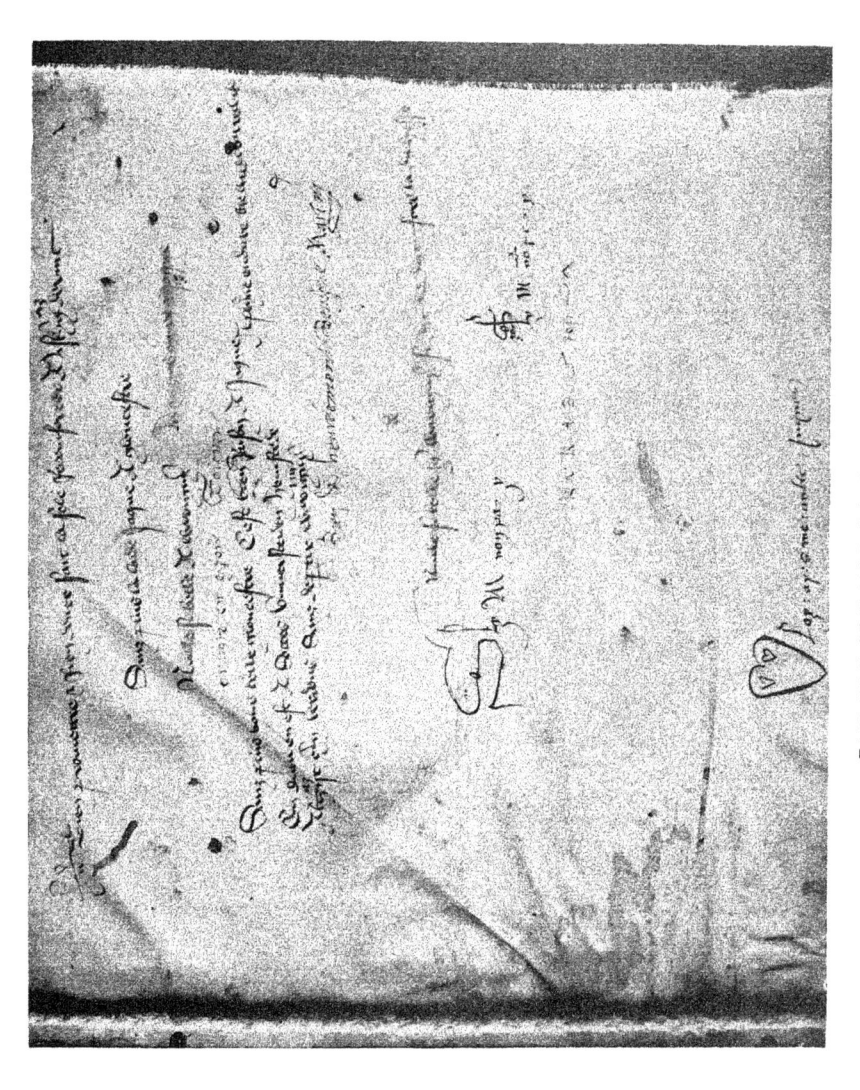

FACSIMILE OF FLY-LEAF IN FROISSART MS.

champ, Earl of Warwick, was acting as regent in France during Bedford's brief absence, fits these phrases fairly well. Just then Jacqueline's fortunes were at a low ebb, and a group of young English people might easily have dared to amuse themselves by making invidious comparisons between her and Madame de Warigny. The first did not need to be ugly, nor the second beautiful, to cause the fickle fancy of Humphrey to swerve from the one to the other so as to cause comment.[1]

The phrases might also have been written in England a few years earlier, and the volume might have been left in Paris in 1439, when its owner, the Earl of Warwick, died there as regent. However they came there, the words have outlived more serious testimony, and the flavour of court gossip is preserved on the fly-leaves.

A *Book of Hours* evidently illuminated for Jacqueline after her fourth marriage gives

---

[1] Löher says that Humphrey was in love with Madame de Wangny, wife of Jacqueline's equerry, and that the latter cherished a romantic devotion to his lady. *Beiträge,* p. 274.

310   A Mediæval Princess

a tiny portrait of her suggesting no beauty in its minuteness.[1] That it was not completed until after her death, is implied by the word *viva* in the inscription, written in most unclassic Latin:

> " Hollandos, Frezones, Zeelandos, Hanoniensis
> Viva regens Jacoba tam comitessa bona
> Bavarie stirpis claris liquet ejus et armis. "

This appears on the miniature of the Annunciation where Jacqueline's kneeling figure is represented. Lord Frank's portrait is in the miniature of the Nativity. The latter bears the following inscription ·

> " Arma gerit suavis comes hic, pariter columpne.
> Franco, decus, norma, caput et flos Borsaliorum
> Juncta thoro Jacoba cui clara fuit comitessa."

In the border of the Annunciation miniature are the figures of the two Saints James. One has a staff and the other a club. The inscription states that these were the patrons

---

[1] In the possession of M. le Comte de Musard. See *Bibliothèque de l'école des chartes*, 1903, pp. 314–320. The book passed from a branch of the Borselens to this French family, who have owned it since 1587. The eleven miniatures are done by different hands.

cherished by the Countess, and again, the past tense, *coluit*, shows that she had already passed out of life when the illuminator finished this page.

The three lines stating that in her lifetime Jacoba of Bavarian stock ruled over Hollanders, Frisians, Zealanders, and Hanonians, and was illustrious from her own deeds of arms, preserve the record of her stormy sovereignty and of her military career, a career that seems inappropriate to the sober, staid, saddened woman, kneeling at her orisons.

The portraits of *Vrau Jacobe* and *Heer Vräck* in the gallery at Amsterdam belong to the same century as their subjects. Possibly the vanished canvas of Jan van Eyck served this unknown artist as a model for the lady's likeness. The head-dress and the contour of the face are very similar to those in the Copenhagen picture. The dress, however, is quite different and bears no trace of the ermine which it was still Jacqueline's privilege to wear when Van Eyck represented her. If the companion portraits were painted after 1436, under Lord Frank's own direction, to commemorate his alliance with the ex-ruler of Holland, he certainly did not insist on a flattering presentment of his personal charms, sufficient though they were to induce his wife to renounce her prouder titles. Possibly his sanctimonious expression is due to the unskilful treatment of the artist, who seems, too, to have used one model for the hands in both portraits

The engraving made for Le Petit's history at the end of the sixteenth century is apparently composed from certain features in the older portraits which were modified to portray a younger woman, imperious, demanding, and still full of the hope which has vanished from the older face.

With Jacqueline's death the Burgundian sovereignty in the Netherlands was assured. A long life was granted to Philip to enjoy the accumulated fruits of his victory. He had the opportunity given by years, an opportunity denied to all the brilliant and

PORTRAIT OF JACQUELINE. CIRCA 1436.
In the National Gallery, Amsterdam.

The Lady and the Land 313

ambitious contemporaries of his youth, whose careers proved too short for the fulfilment of their dreams.

In the struggle for supremacy the burghers of the contested provinces won many advantages given as bribes for the allegiance of their towns. When Philip was firmly established he repudiated his grants and had no hesitation in employing there the same autocratic methods to which other portions of his domain were accustomed. But the fact of their sometime possession of privileges was never forgotten by the Hollanders. When the later issue was made between the overlord and the cities, the demand was not for novel and unknown liberties but for their former charters. A golden era of civic individuality was set up as a standard whose brief and shadowy existence was fondly cherished.

It must be remembered that under the Counts of Holland, the provinces were feudal estates, allied only because the headship happened to be vested in one person. Philip's hand welded the separate and incongruous parts together and forced them to be members of one body—a Burgundian state. Under the outward unity, burgher life grew in the communities, that obeyed but still held tenaciously to a latent spark of independence, to a national spirit, typified by the last Daughter of Holland.

BIBLIOGRAPHY

The sources for general Netherland history in the fifteenth century, and later works based thereon, are discussed by Prof. P. J. Blok, *Geschiedenis van het Nederlandsche, Volk. II.*, *Aanhangsel;* English version, *A History of the People of the Netherlands*, ii., pp. 389-406 (New York, 1899). See also *Eene Hollandsche Stad in de Middeleeuwen*, by the same author (s'Gravenhage, 1883).

For a closer study of the period, the best basis is the chapter on sources in *Jakobäa und Ihre Zeit.* Franz von Löher. Nordlingen, 2 vols., 1867. I., pp. 403-430.

In his own narrative Löher is somewhat sentimental, but in his investigation of historical material his industry has been extraordinary. His list of sources must, however, be supplemented for all publications later than 1867, and many documents have been rendered available since then.

The *Dictionary of National Biography* (vol. xxviii.) should also be consulted; and the *Bibliographie de l'histoire de Belgique* (H. Pirenne, 2d edition; Brussels, 1902).

The following list comprises simply the chief works drawn upon for contemporaneous material, either printed intact or quoted, and a few later works specifically cited. Many others both in English and French are useful.

Documents:

Groot Charterboek der Graven van Holland van Zeeland en Heeren van Vriesland verzaameld en in orde gebragt door Frans van Mieris. Leyden, 1733. 4 vols. This collection contains documents from the earliest times to the death of our "Countess, Vrouwe Jacoba van Beijere." The editor was an artist, not a scholar, and his work is not critical and is marred by omissions. Fischer, de Jonghe, Kluit, and various historical associations have published many documents of whose existence Van Mieris was ignorant. Although more than a thousand documents relating to Jacqueline are printed in vol. iv., they must be supplemented from other sources.

Groot Placaat Boek. Ordinances, etc., of the States-General. Ed., Cornelis Cau. s'Gravenhage, 1683. Vol. iii. contains some documents not found elsewhere.

Cartulaire des Comtes de Hainaut de l'avènement de Guillaume II., à la mort de Jacqueline de Bavière. Publié par Leopold Devillers (Bruxelles, 1881–92). Vols. iv. and v. contain much important matter, deeds, letters, extracts from city registers, etc.

Particularités Curieuses sur Jacqueline de Bavière, Comtesse de Hainaut et sur le Comté de Hainaut. Extraits des registres des résolutions du conseil de la ville de Mons. 2 vols. Vol. i. edited by A. D. (Mons, 1838). Vol. ii. edited by Leopold Devillers (Mons, 1879). (Soc. des Bibliophiles Belges.)

Devillers, Leopold. *Inventaire Analytique des Archives de la ville de Mons.* Part I. (Mons, 1882–96).

In the Royal Library at Brussels, under No. 9976, there is a collection of documents entitled *Processus inter Johannem ducem Brabantiæ et Jacobam de Bavaria.* The most important of these were used by Edmund Dynter. See under Chroniclers of the fifteenth century.

Fœdera Conventiones Literæ et Cujuscumque Generis Acta Publica inter Reges Angliæ et Alios. Thomas Rymer, editor. Vol. x. contains various acts relating to Jacqueline's English marriage (2d edition, London, 1727). See also *Fœdera,* syllabus of vols. ii. and iii., ed., Th. D. Hardy (London).

Calendar of Patent Rolls. Preserved in the Public Record Office. Henry VI, A.D. 1422–29. Ed., A. Hughes (London, 1901).

Proceedings and Ordinances of the Privy Council of England. Edited by Sir Harris Nicolas (London, 1835). Vols. ii., iii., iv.

The Paston Letters (1422–1509). Ed. James Gairdner (London, 1872).

Letters and Papers Illustrative of the Wars of the English in France during the Reign of Henry VI. 3 vols. Ed. Rev. Joseph Stevenson. ("Master of Rolls" Series.) London, 1864.

Collections (Society and Periodical):

Historische Genootschap te Utrecht. The publications of this Society contain many studies on particular topics, such as Court expenditures and accounts, etc.; also many documents, such as the reckoning of Jacqueline's executors, etc. *Kroniek*, see 1850–51–52–60, etc.; *Codex diplomaticus*, see 1852–53, etc.; also *Bijdragen en Mededeelingen, Berigten*, and *Werken* (five series in all). Utrecht, 1846–1903.

Abhandlungen der Historischen Classe der Königlich Bayerischen Akademie der Wissenschaften. Munchen, 1867. Vol. x. *Beitrage zur Geschichte der Jakobaa von Bayern* (*Erste Abtheilung*, p. 1; *Zweite Abtheilung*, p. 205). These articles contain extracts from much unprinted material; and two complete MS. histories, designated *Codex Tegernseer* and *The Hague Codex*.

Bijdragen voor Vaderlandsche Geschiedenis en Oudheidkunde. Editors: J. A. Nijhoff and P. Nijhoff; later, Dr. Fruin, Dr. Blok, and Dr. Muller. (Four series.) The Hague, 1837–1904. See Nos. 1 and 2; New Series, No. 6; Third Series, Nos. 2 and 8, etc. Certain of these valuable articles are now reprinted in Fruin's collected works.

Mémoires couronnés et autres Mémoires. Publiés par l'Académie Royale de Belgique, Bruxelles. Vol. xxi., 1881. *Geschiedenis van Jacoba van Beieren*. Frans de Potter. Many records reprinted. See other volumes of the series; see also *Journal des Savants* (Paris, 1899); *Bibliothèque de l'École des Chartes* (Paris, 1903, lxiv.). Other local collections should also be consulted under names of cities and provinces.

Chronicles by authors of fifteenth century (French and Netherland)

Froissart, Jean (b. 1337, d. 1410?). *Chroniques de France, d'Angleterre, d' Écosse, d'Espagne, de Flandres*. 26 vols. Ed. Kervyn de Lettenhove (Bruxelles, 1867–77). The English translation used is that by Sir John Bourchier, Lord Berners (1523–25); reprint, 1901.

Froissart, himself a native of Valenciennes, is a valuable authority for the times of Count William VI and for the last years before Jacqueline's birth.

Dynter, Edmund de (d. 1448). *Chronica nobilissimorum ducum Lotharingiæ et Brabantiæ ac regum Francorum auctore magistro Edmundo de Dynter. Liber VI.* Series *Chroniques Belges.* Bruxelles, 1857.

The rector of the University of Louvain, P. F. X. De Ram, brought out an edition of this chronicle with the addition of a French translation by Jean Wauquelin Edmund de Dynter was private secretary to John IV of Brabant, and to Philip of Burgundy. He had many opportunities to know the inner history of the Court of Brabant, as he was frequently employed on confidential business. In 1417 he assisted in the negotiations for Jacqueline's marriage. Very often, however, his testimony in regard to her is of little value, as he wrote at the behest of Philip of Burgundy and coloured his statements to suit his patron. The great value of his work is that he had access to state papers and archives, and incorporated many into his text. At the same time, as he omits what might displease Philip, his narrative must be supplemented in many places. He states that he is induced to write of the wars between Jacqueline and her cousins because many talk much (*multi multum loquuntus*), and the assertions of the wicked prevent truth coming to light. He hopes that when his words are read, the world's eyes shall never again be darkened by falsification.

De Brabantsche Yēēsten of Rijmkronijk van Braband. Derde deel. Edited by J. H. Bormans. (*Chroniques Belges.*) Bruxelles, 1869. See Book VII.

This rhymed narrative of the deeds of the dukes of Brabant consists of two parts. The first, by Jean le Clerc, or Jean de Boendale, was finished c. 1350. The continuation, which alone concerns our Jacqueline, was finished 1440, by an unknown author. He himself states that he was in the service of John of Brabant. After describing the Duke's death, 1427, he adds:

"And above all so was he
By his servants, be it said to you
Unspeakably bewailed.
I speak but true, ah me, with right.
I was his servant and his knave;
The noble dear and good my lord
Gave me in so many hours
So many sweet words with his mouth.
That throughout my whole life
They will be printed on my heart.

The seventh book of this anonymous Brabanter covers the ground of Dynter's sixth, and seems to be either a rhymed version in the vernacular of the Latin history, or based on material used by Dynter.

Le Fevre, Jean, Seigneur de St. Rémy (b. 1395, d. 1463). *Chronique.* (Soc. de l' Hist. de France. Ed. F. Morand. 2 vols. Paris, 1876.)

St. Rémy was at the battle of Agincourt with Jehan de Waurin. Later, he was king-at-arms of Philip of Burgundy, and was called *Toison d'Or.* He was at Agincourt, accompanied Philip on various campaigns, and made many journeys into foreign lands until he was too ill to travel. Then he devoted himself to writing down his recollections, copying freely from Monstrelet, or perhaps exchanging with him. Certainly he adds many personal bits. For instance, he is the only author who makes Jacqueline jealous of John of Brabant. He says that the devil interfered when she went to England.

Monstrelet, Enguerrand de (d. 1453). *La Chronique* (1400–1444). (Soc .de l'Hist. de France. Paris, 1861. Ed. L. Douët D'Arcq.) Vol. iv.

Monstrelet continued Froissart's chronicles with diminished charm, but increased critical faculty. At the time of writing he was a magistrate in Cambray. Burgundian in sympathies, he was still less vehemently partisan than other writers. He uses many originals that have now disappeared. Rabelais calls him " slobbering."

Chastellain, Georges (b. 1405, d. 1475). *Chronique.* Ed. Kervyn de Lettenhove. Brussels, 1863. (Academie Royale de Belgique.)

The author was a jurist of Ghent, privy councillor to Philip and on a confidential footing with him. There is great charm in the style of this chronicle, which contains much about the early years of Jacqueline. Unfortunately the MS. for the periods 1422–1430, 1431–1452, has never been found.

La declaration de tous les hauts faits et glorieuses adventures du duc Philippe de Bourgogne also contains some disparagement of Jacqueline in eulogising her cousin.

Fenin, Pierre de (d. 1433). *Mémoires* (1407–1427). 1 vol. Ed. Dupont. Paris, 1837.

In the main, Fenin copies Monstrelet or his sources in his account of the wars of Burgundy. His style is poor, but he is valuable for some facts not found elsewhere.

Waurin, Jehan de, Seigneur de Forestel (b., c. 1394, d., c. 1474). *Recueil des Chroniques et Anchiennes Istories de la Grant Bretagne à présent nommé Engleterre* (vol. v., 1422–1431). ("Master of the Rolls" Series. Ed. Wm. Hardy. London, 1879.)

Not many details are known about this author, who wrote his history late in life, after he was forced to give up active service. He drew freely from all other chronicles, in some cases acknowledging his sources.

Journal d'un Bourgeois de Paris. Michaud et Poujoulat. Col. des Mémoires pour servir à l'histoire de France, xii.

Marche, Olivier de la (b. 1422). *Mémoires.* Lyon, 1562.

He was page in Philip's court at thirteen, and remained there until his old age, when he was High Court Master. He knew the duke's character well, and is interesting for the period, though he says little of Jacqueline directly.

Cronique de Flandre, par auteur incertain. Ed. Denis Sauvage. Lyon, 1562. (Bound in same volume with La Marche.)

Les chroniques des pays de Hollande, Zeelande, et aussi en parties de Haynnau. Comte-rendu des séances de la commission royale. Bruxelles, 1887.

Potter, Dirc. *Der Minnen Loep.* Ed. P. Leendertz, Wz. Leyden, 1845.

The author was court secretary in Holland, 1402–1428.

Bibliography

In addition to the above, there were many other French-Burgundian chroniclers between Froissart and Comines who touch more or less on the affairs of the Netherlands. Those mentioned borrow from each other, yet all have some originality in their work and must be read to supplement each other. In all cases documents were incorporated more or less accurately into their narratives. Chronological and other errors of various kinds abound and must be corrected by other data.

(English):

Capgrave, John (b. 1393). *The Chronicle of England.* Ed. Rev. F. C. Hingeston, B.A. ("Master of Rolls" Series. London, 1858.)

The Book of the Illustrious Henries. Trans. from the Latin by Rev. F. C. Hingeston, M.A. ("Master of Rolls" Series. London, 1858.)

Hardynge, John (b. 1378, d., c. 1465). *The Chronicle of English History.* Ed. Henry Ellis. London, 1812.

    The author of this rhymed history was with the English army in France, and possibly with Henry V at the time of his death.

Henrici Quinti Regis Angliæ Gesta auctore capellano in exercitu regio. Ed. Benjamin Williams. London, 1850.

Chronica Monasterii S. Albani. *Annales.* A Johanne Amundesham—monacho. *Chronicon, a quodam auctore ignoto compilatum.* Ed. Henry Thomas Riley. ("Master of Rolls" Series. London, 1870.)

Later chronicles cited in text:

Stow, John. *Annales; or, A Generall Chronicle of England,* begun by John Stow and continued by Edmund Howes, Gent. London, 1631.

Holinshed, Raphael. *The Historie of England.* 3 vols. London, 1576.

Grimeston, Ed. *A Generall Historie of the Netherlands* continued from the year 1608 till the year of our Lord 1627, by William Crosse. London, 1627.

Bibliography

Meyer, Jacob (Jacobus de Meyerus) (b. 1491). *Rerum Flandricarum Annales.* Bruges, 1842.

Gouthoven, W. van. *D'oude Chronijcke ende Historie van Holland, 1449–1636.* s'Gravenhage, 1636.

Velius, D. *Chronik van Hoorn.* Hoorn, 1648.

Vinchant, François (d. 1635). *Annales de la province et Comté de Hainaut.* 6 vols.

Le Petit, Jean François. *La Grande Chronique de Hollande Zelande, West Frise, etc., jusques à la fin de l'an 1600.* 2 vols. Dordrecht, 1601.

For the debts of the Dutch chroniclers to each other see *Bijdragen*, 1875, p. 347.

INDEX

A

Abele, Floris van, 263, 281
Agincourt, battle of, 16
Albert, Count. *See* Holland
Alfen, battles of, 163, 175
Amersfort, 161
Amsterdam, 30, 164, 311
Antwerp, 154, 303; Margravate of, 58
d'Arc, Jeanne, 216, 217; death of, 254
Arent of Ghent, 218
Arkel, William of, 15, etc.; death of, 40
Arkels, the, 34, 57, etc.
Armagnacs, the, 13
Arnold of Ghent, 184, 205
Arras, Treaty of, 255, 256
Artois, Bonne of, Duchess of Burgundy, 152
d'Asche, Laurette, 61
Ath, 145

B

Baest, Leon de, 50
Barante, *Histoire des Ducs de Bourgogne* quoted 37, 170 *et passim*
Baudon, Jacquemars 77
Baugé, battle of, 89
Bavaria, family of, 1
Bavaria, Albert of, Count of Holland. *See* Holland Zealand and Hainaut
Bavaria, Jacqueline of, 3, 209. *See* Jacqueline

Bavaria, John of (the Pitiless), Bishop-elect of Liége, 6, 10, 18, *et passim;* character of, 36, 37; heads Cod opposition to Jacqueline, 39, 40; opposes Brabant marriage, 41–43, 48, 52; marriage of, 50, 53; acknowledged heir to Jacqueline, 56, 57, 87, etc.; success of, 102; death of 118–121

Bavaria, Lewis of, 1, 2

Bavaria, William of, 1, 15. *See* William IV and William VI

Beaufort, Cardinal, 254. *See* Winchester

Bedford, John, Duke of, 44 *et passim*, 86, 92, 93, 131; character of, 97; marries Anne of Burgundy, 104; prevents duel between Burgundy and Gloucester, 158–160; efforts of, to maintain Burgundian alliance, 197, 198, *et passim·* marries Jacquet of Luxemburg, 253, 254; death of, 255

Beguines, the, 263, 268, 298

Benedict XIII (Pedro da Luna), 94

Beukels, Jan, 32

Beylinck, Arnold (or Allaert), 178

Biervliet, Council of, 36, 168

Bilderdijk, quoted, 58, 221, 249

Bleeswijc, Bartelmeus van, 279

Blondel, William, 47

Blouncell, John, 89

Boendale, Jan van, *Brabantsche Yeesten* 16

Bois-le-Duc, 134

Bologna, Cardinal of, 200

Borselen, Floris van, 120, etc.

Borselen, Frank van, 120, 172; appointed stadtholder of Holland, etc., 218, 219, 233; description of, 219, 220; aids Jacqueline, 223, 224; marries Jacqueline, 226, 244, 245; imprisonment of, 227–230, 236, 240; pension settled on, 242; made Count of Ostrevant, 245–247, 262, 266, 269; portraits of, 310, 311

Bouchain, 14, 17, 70, 80, 113, 290, 299

Bouchout, Daniel de, 133

Brabant, Three Estates of, 185

Brabant, Anthony, Duke of, 16

Brabant, John IV, Duke of, 16, 18; marriage negotiations of, 36–38; opposition to marriage of, 41–43, 48; papal dispensation for marriage of, granted, 41, 50; marriage of

Index

Brabant—*Continued*
  celebrated, 45–48; treaties of, with John of Bavaria, 56–59, 67, 68; character of, 60–62; treatment of Jacqueline by, 62–67; Jacqueline leaves, 67, 69, 96; willing to accept arbitration, 105, 106; willing to renounce Jacqueline, 109; dispossessed as Count of Hainaut, 116, 117; takes possession of Holland, 122, 123; divorce of, pending, 135; restored to sovereignty of Hainaut, 144, 146; appoints Duke of Burgundy ruward, 150; death of, 184–186, 261; title of, 186; University of Louvain founded by, 186

Brabantsche Yeesten, quoted, 16, 63, 170, *et passim*
Braine-le-Comte, surrender of, 133, 136
Breda, 155
Brederode, 198
Bremmont, Amand de, 50
Brill, 162, 239
Brouwershaven, battle at, 167, 172 180
Bruges, 206, 232
Brunelleschi, 300
Brussels, 20, 185, 215, 234, 281
Bruweliis, Simon van, 4
Bruyn, Jan de, 267
Burgundy, Anne of, Duchess of Bedford, 87, 104, 152; death of, 253
Burgundy, House of, 242
Burgundy, John (the Fearless), Count of Flanders, Duke of 18, 36, 46, 56
Burgundy, Margaret of, Countess of Holland, 1–3, etc. *See* Holland
Burgundy, Philip (Count of Charolais), Duke of, 56, 77; intervention of, in Jacqueline's affairs, 77–79; ambition of, 87, 88; refuses to acknowledge legality of Jacqueline's divorce, 92, 104; aids John of Brabant, 117, 124, 125, 134; letters of, to Gloucester, 127, 128, 131; challenges Gloucester, 128; ruward and heir of Holland, 150, 161, 163, 171; wins battle of Brouwershaven, 167–171; Hainaut accepts government of, 188–190; forces Jacqueline to sign Treaty of Delft, 206–209; makes progress throughout provinces with Jacqueline, 209, 210; in Paris, 215,

Burgundy—*Continued*
216; hears of Jacqueline's marriage, 226; imprisons Borselen, 227; forces Jacqueline to abdicate, 229, 236, *et seq.;* obtains possession of Namur and Brabant, 230, 231; marriage of, with Isabel of Portugal, 232, 240, 304; institutes Order of Golden Fleece, 232; plot against life of, 234; makes second progress with Jacqueline, 241, 242; sanctions Jacqueline's marriage with Van Borselen, 244, 245; birth of Charles the Bold, 246; acknowledges Charles VII King of France, 255, 256; Van Eyck in employ of, 303, 304

Bye, William de, 223, 224

Calais, 80, 112, 256, 300
Cambge, Guillaume du, 79
Cambray, 185
Charles VI, King of France, 3, 88, 92
Charles VII, King of France, 255. *See* Dauphin
Charolais, Philip, Count of, 36, 56. *See* Burgundy
Chastellain, Georges, quoted, 78, 304, *et passim*
Clarence, Duke of, 89
Cobham, Eleanor, relations of, with Duke of Gloucester, 137, 201–204; marriage of, 205; convicted of witchcraft, 259–261
Cocqueau quoted, 84
Codex Tegernseer, the, 226, 235, *et passim*
Cods, the, 122, 157, 162, 164, 167, 189, 208, 234, 235
Cologne, 187, 278
Compiègne, 3, 5, 12, 13, 254
Constance, Council of, 40–42, 48, 50
Copenhagen, 301, 304, 311
Cortgene (Borselen), Philip of, 120, 218, 233
Crespin, 113, 137
Croy, Anthony de, 244

D

Damme, 271
Dauphin, the (John of Touraine), 9, 11–14; (Charles VII) 88, 89, 158, 199, 216

Delft, 30, etc.; Treaty of, 206, 209, 210, 226, 253, 304; provisions of Treaty of, 206–208
Der Minnen Loep, 290
Deventer, 295
Dordrecht, 20, 39, 53, 86, 123, 166, 263, 274
Dorp, Philip van, treasurer of Holland, 4, 5
Douay, 14
Douls, Simons li, 95
Dover, 82, 86, 111, 300
Duivenvoorde, Dietrich van, 269
Dynter, Edmund de, quoted, 43, 65, 94, 116, 169, 184–186 *et passim*

E

Egmont, William van, 263
Egmonts, the, 34, 57
England, 9, etc., 196, 235, 287, 306, *et passim*
Enkhuizen, 33
Everyman, 292

F

Faucille, Victor de la, 156
Féron, Jaquemart le, 112
Fitzwater, Lord, 165, 166, 169
Flanders, 228
Flanders, Count of, 18, *see* Burgundy. Title of, 256 258
Flushing, Ludwig of, 30
Friesland, 102, 208, 288, 289
Friesland, countship of, 237
Froissart, Sir John, quoted, 284 *et seq.*; MS. vol. of, 305–308
Fuhr, 63

G

Gaesbeck, 168
Geertruidenberg, 110, 293
Ghent, 20, 152, 153, 233
Gijsbrecht of Amsterdam, 263, 268
Gillis, Master, 263, 268
Gloucester, Humphrey, Duke of, meeting of, with Jacqueline 82, 86; proposed marriage of, with Anne of Burgundy, 87; sent to France, 88, 89; marries Jacqueline, 93–95;

Gloucester—*Continued*
    character of, 97; learning of, 97–99; gifts to Oxford, 98
    appeals for aid to Duke of Burgundy, 104; letters of, to
    Philip of Burgundy, 125–131; accepts Philip's challenge
    130, 131; returns to England, 136, 137; postpones duel
    144; consents to arbitration, 106, 107; efforts of, to
    have marriage proved valid, 109, 181, 182; raises force to
    take possession of Hainaut, 111; recognised as Count of
    Hainaut, 116; promises aid to Jacqueline, 157; send
    troops under Lord Fitzwater, 165, 166; defeat of troop
    at Brouwershaven, 167, 169–171; Papal decision in re
    gard to marriage, 200, 203; petition to, in behalf of
    Jacqueline, 203, 204; marries Eleanor Cobham, 205, 259
    260; saves Calais, 256; death of, 260; persecution of
    Lollards by, 299
Goes, 220, 269
Golden Fleece, Order of the, instituted, 232, etc.
Gonengiis, Gilliis van, 4
Gorcum, 39, etc., 56, 240
Gorlitz, Elizabeth of, 50, 53, 148, 223
Gouda, 32, 156, 157, 161, 164, 168, 177, 183, 206
Grafenstein, fortress of the, 147, 153
Grenier, Jan or Jean, 192, 193, 264, 280
Grimeston, Edward, English historian, 230
Groot Charterboek, the, edited by Van Mieris, 54 *et passim*
Groot, Gerard de, 295
Guilbant, Guy, 244

H

Haarlem, 30, 164, 281; siege of, 174, 175
Haarlem, Jan of, 296
Hague, The, 1, 8, *et passim*, 103, 111, 120, 236, 247, 265, 26
    290
Hainaut, 188, 196, 208, 210, 217, 232, 234, *et passim*
Hainaut, Count of, 1, 52, 96, 105, 106, 108, 116, 257
Hainaut, countship of, 54, 109, 237
Hainaut, Estates of, 73 *et passim*, 95, 96, 114, 116, 188
Hainaut and Holland contrasted, 20
Hainaut, Philippa of, 78
Hal, 95, 110, 116

Index

Hameide, Mme. de, 47
Harpre, Marie de, 72
Hartford (Hardfort), 95
Haucin, Willaumes de, 14
Havré, lord of, 116
Hearne, quoted, 98
Heerenthals, 58
Henry IV, King of England, 44, 256
Henry V, King of England, 44, 79, 82, 88, 92, 93, 97
Henry VI, King of England and of France, 91, 92, 104, 105, 192, 194, 255–259
Heusden, 110
Hildegaersberch, William van, 290–292, 294
Hokelen, Jan of, 296
Holland, 161, 171, 180, 188, 196, 208, 210, 217, 219, 232, 235, *et passim;* education in, 295 *et seq.;* religious conditions in, 299
Holland, Albert of Bavaria, Count of, 1, 285, 288, 295
Holland, Count of, 257, 258, 295, *et passim;* countship of, 2, 54, 237, 239
Holland, Daughter of, *see* Jacqueline
Holland, Jacqueline, Countess of, *see* Jacqueline
Holland, Margaret of Burgundy, Countess of, 3, 15, 17, 44, 66, 76, 85, 209, 231, 232, 264, 269, 289
Holland, Son of, 1, 58
Holland, William IV, Count of, *see* William IV
Holland, Zealand, and Hainaut, William VI (Count of Ostrevant), Count of, 1–3, 14, 102, *see also* William VI
Hoogtwoude, Eberhard of, 30
Hooks, 153, 157, 160–163, 166, 167, 171, 208, 234, 235
Hoorn, 33, 177–179
Humphrey, Duke of Gloucester. *See* Gloucester
Huss, John, 40

I

Isabelle, Queen of France, 11

J

Jacoba. *See* Jacqueline
Jacoba's Preeltje, 269

Index

Jacqueline, Countess of Holland, Zealand, etc., birth of, 1; Daughter of Holland, 1, 9, 17, 283, 314; various names of, 2, 3, 189, 191, 265; betrothal of, to Duke of Touraine 3–6; titles of, 5, 9, 14, 67, 95, 99, 102, 207, 209, 239, 246, 283; Papal dispensation required for marriage of, 8; marriage of, celebrated, 8, 279; Dauphiness of Vienne, 9, 283; death of Dauphin, 13; proposed husband for, 15, 16, 40; death of William VI, 17; takes oath of sovereignty, 19, 24; receives homage, 19–29, 220; character of, 19, 35, 85; Cod opposition to, in Holland, 29–34, 39; proposed marriage of, with Duke of Brabant, 36–38; Papal dispensation for Brabant marriage, 37, 40, 41; opposition of John of Bavaria to, 39–43; wins battle at Gorcum, 39; generosity of, 38, 70–72, 209, 217, 218, 253; marriage dispensations revoked, 43, 50, 51, 76; Duke of Bedford proposed as husban for, 44, 86; married to Duke of Brabant, 45–48; progress of, through Hainaut and Brabant, 53; at war with John of Bavaria, 53–55; lands of, mortgaged to John of Bavaria, 56–59, 67, 68; unhappy marriage of, 60 *et seq.*; flees from Brabant, 67, 69, 73; declares her marriage illegal, 75, 76; fears intervention of Philip, 77, 78; seeks refuge in England, 78, 80–85, 300, 301; meets Duke of Gloucester, 82, 86; kindness of Henry V to, 89, 90; declares Brabant marriage null and void, 91, 92, 109, 114, 115, 260; god-mother to Henry VI, 92; married to Duke of Gloucester, 93–96; acknowledged in England as Duchess of Gloucester, 99–101, 106; naturalised in England, 104, 105; consents to arbitration, 107, 108; her divorce not decided, 108–110, 112, 135; proceeds to Hainaut with Humphrey, 111–114; Estates recognise Humphrey as Count of Hainaut, 116; Burgundy aids Brabant against, 117 *et seq.*; Brabant league against, 134 bids farewell to Humphrey, 137; appeals to Council o Mons, 137; letter of, to Gloucester, 138–142; letter of to Count Palatine, 142, 143; delivered up to guardian ship of Burgundy, 145; imprisonment of, 147, 150, 152 escapes from Ghent, 153–156, 301; establishes head quarters at Gouda, 157; Gloucester promises aid to, 157 162; victorious at Alfen, 163, 164, 175; Humphrey send troops, 165, 166; English fleet captured, 167, 168; ovei

Jacqueline—*Continued*
    whelming defeat of, at Brouwershaven, 169–171; loses all foothold in Zealand, 172; stories of severity of, 176–178; validity of marriage with Gloucester still undecided, 181; effect of Papal bulls on adherents of, 183; appeals to Privy Council of England, 183, 184, 191–194; protests against Burgundy's usurpation of power, 188–191; English aid promised to, 194–196; Brabant marriage declared valid, 200; appeals against Papal decision, 200; Gloucester faithless to, 200, 201; pent up in Gouda, 206; signs Treaty of Delft, 206–209; makes progress with Burgundy throughout provinces, 209–211, 301; signs new treaty with Burgundy, 213; takes up abode at The Hague, 217; meets Van Borselen, 221–225; secret marriage of, 226; Burgundy forces abdication of 229, 230, 236–238, 301; Countess of Ostrevant, 239, 241, 244, 262; position of Burgundy and, reversed, 240; makes second progress with Philip, 241, 242; letters of, announcing her abdication, 243; secret compact with Philip, 243; public marriage of, with Van Borselen, 245; made Lady Forester, 246; legends relating to, 247–249; patron of art and letters, 250, 252, 253; wardrobe of 251, 275; jewels of, 251, 280; letter of Henry VI to, 257, 258; illness and death of, 261–264; will of, 264; burial of, 265, 266; expense of obsequies, 266 *et seq.;* effigy of, 268, 269; sale of effects of, 274–276; bequests of, 276 *et seq.*, 299; characteristics of, 282, 283, 292, 299, 300; portraits of, 283, 284, 301–304, 310, 311; education of, 293, 294; *Book of Hours* belonging to, 309–311

Jeumont, Lord of, 114
Joan (Joanna), Queen of England, 90, 101
John IV, of Brabant. *See* Brabant
John XXIII, Pope, 7, 8
Jordan, Marjory, the Witch of Eye, 201, 259
Joris, the sculptor, 268

K

Kannetjes, Vrouw Jacoba's, story of, 248–250
Kennemerland, 33 *et passim,* 182

Knuypf, Jan, 177
Knuypf, Lambert, 177
Kyfhoek, Floris van, 263, 281

L

Lalain, Mme. de, 47
Lancaster, Duchy of, 196
Lancaster, Henry of, 78, 287, etc.
Langley, 101, 301
Lannoy, Hugo van, stadtholder of Holland and Zealand 242
Leeds, 307
Leerdam, 56
Le Grand, Gérard, 138
Leiderdorp, 263
Le Petit, François, 312
Leyden, 30, 164, 166, 198, 295, 297, 299
Leyden, John of, 263, 268
Leyot, Richard, 44
Lille, 152, 194, 209, 238
Loge, Jehan de le, 112
Löher, Franz von, quoted, 42 *et passim*, 293
Lollards, the, 299
London, 166, 285, 289, 300
London, Bishop of, 159
Louis, Count Palatine, 142
Louvain, University of, founded, 186, 187
Luxemburg, 148
Luxemburg, Jacquet of, Duchess of Bedford 253, 254
Luxemburg, John of, 146, 163, 254
Lydgate, John, quoted, 97, 308

M

Maas, the, 167
Macart, Sergeant, 140
Martin, Master, 263
Martin V, Pope, grants dispensation for Brabant marriage, 40, 41; revokes dispensation, 43; revokes revocation, 50, 76, 109; delay in settling divorce, 94, 108, 135, 136, 183; grants privileges to University of Louvain, 187; declares validity of Brabant marriage, 199, 200

Mauberge, 116
Medemblik, 33
Medemblik, William of, 30
Mezeray, quoted, 36
Mije, Jan van der, 270, 281
Mirror, the, inn at Brussels 67
Monnikendam, 33
Mons, 6, etc., 19, 70, 84, 95, 138, 144–146, 190, 210, 217, 299
Mons, Adolph, Duke of, 46
Monstrelet, Enguerrand, quoted 44 *et passim*, 125, 235, 304
Montereau, 77
Montfort, Louis de, 140, 141, 184
Mont Saint Martin, Mme. de, 47
Musard, Comte de, 310
Muyden, 161

N

Naarden, 161
Naasterhof, 113
Namur, 148
Namur, John III., Count of, 230, 231
Nassau, Count of, 144, 172
Netherlands, the, pass over to House of Burgundy, 242 312
Noordwijk, 232, 234
Nothaft, Henry, 302

O

"Ooltgens," the, 280
Orange, Prince of, 145
l'Orfevre, Jan, 114
Orleans, Isabella of, 5
Orleans, Maid of. *See* Jeanne d'Arc
Orleans, siege of, 215, 216, 254
Ostende, 220, etc.
Ostrevant, Count of, 1, 245–247, 284. *See* under Holland, William VI
Ostrevant, Countess of, 239, 241, 244, 262. *See* Jacqueline
Otto the Great, Emperor, 147
Oudewater, 32, 161

P

Papendrecht, 55
Paris, 12, etc., 112, 187, 215, 216, 255, 289, 305, 309
Paris, University of, 132
Paston, William, *Letters* of, 181
Percy, Lord Thomas, 307
Poelgeest, Gerard de, 81
Pope John XXIII, 8
Pope Martin V. *See* Martin
Portugal, 304
Portugal, Isabel of, Duchess of Burgundy, 232, 234, 240, 304
Postelles, Ægidius, 234
Potter, Dirc, 290, 291
Potter, Gerard, 265, 267, 281, 293
Poulés, Gilles, 95
Poulette, Agnes, 71
Puche, Andriu, 95
Purmerende, 119
Puyctinck, Jan, 272

Q

Quesnoy (Le Quesnoy), 6, 72, 112, 116, 234, 290

R

Rasoir, Jan, 67
Rheims, 255
Richard II, King of England, 287, 306–308
Rietuelt, Ermgart van, 275
Robessart, John, Seigneur of Escaillon, 78, 101, 105
Rotselaer, Lord John of, etc., 185
Rotterdam, 56, 167
Rupelmonde, 228, 229, 236
Ruyschrock, Jan, 218, 271

S

Salisbury, Duke of, 215
St. Albans, 99, 203, 259, 301
St Catherine's Day, 236

Index

St. George's Day, 131, 136
St. Ghislain, 137
St. Jacques, Hospital, 217
St. James, 80
St. James's Day, 1, 68, 260
St. Martensdijk, 245, 247, 264, 265, 267
Saint-Mor des Fossez, 13
St. Paul's Cross, 260
St. Pol, Philip, Count of, 55, 133, 185; becomes Duke of Brabant, 199, 231
St. Remy, Seigneur de, 211
St. Waltrude, Church of (Wandru-Waltrudis), 24, 189, 210
Savoy, 152
Scheldt, the, 229
Schoonhoven, 39, 118, 123, 157, 161, 179
Senlis, 11.
Sigismund, Emperor, 9, 42, 48, etc., 86, 179, 180
Sluis, 151
Smit, Brother Heynric, 267
Soignies, 63, 116
Soutberg, John of, 219
Spierinck, Arnold, 153
Steynkerke, Mme. de, 47
Stow, John, quoted, 92, 203, 204
Sturmy, William, 44
Sutton, Robert, 181
Sylvius, Æneas, quoted, 201

T

Ternant, Lord Philip de, 227
Texel, 198
Teylingen, 33, 247, 249, 263
Touraine, John, Duke of, betrothed to Jacqueline, 3-5; marriage of, 7, 279; becomes Dauphin, 9, 12; death of, 13
Touraine, Duchess of, 5-7, 279, 283. *See* Jacqueline
Tournay, Bishop of, 46, 159
Troyes, Treaty of, 88, 205
T'serclaes, Everhard, 61
Tudor, Owen, 226

U

Utrecht, 35, 161
Utrecht, Bishop of, 46
Uutkerke, Jehan van, 175
Uutkerke, Roeland van, 171

V

Valenciennes, 7, 20, 29, 80, 116, 190, 214
Valois, Catherine of, 90, 93, 226
Van den Does, Mlle., 47
Van der Poele, Mlle., 47
Van der Berg, Willem, treasurer of Brabant, 61, 276
Van Eyck, Jan, 103, 147, 252, 301, 302, 304, 311
Van Mieris, Frans, quoted, 54 *et passim*, 238
Van Vliet, Beatrice, 4, 30, 118
Van Vliet, Jan (or John), 30, 118
Vere, 239
Vianen, 155, 158
Vianen, Henry, Lord of, 155
Vienne, Dauphiness of, 9, 283
Vilain, Jean de, 170
Vilvoorde, 63, 185
Vinchant, François, quoted, 304 *et passim*

W

Wagenaar, Jan, quoted, 93
Warigny, Madame de, 309
Warwick, Richard de Beauchamp, Earl of, 308, 309
Wassenaar, Dirk van, 295
Wassenaar, Lord of, 32, 34
Waurin, Jehan de, quoted, 202, 206
Westminister, 260
Wieringen, 198
Willesme, Pierart, 71
William IV (of Bavaria), Count of Holland, 1, 2, 289
William VI (of Bavaria), Count of Holland, 1, 3, 8, *et seq.;* in England, 10, 284, *et seq.;* in Paris, 11–13, 289; illness and death of, 14–17, 235; in Friesland, 289; court of, 284, 290–292; character of, 290